THE MAGIC MAN

PETER OF MYSTIC MOUNTAIN

Blessed Mama & Mame, may you be filled with joy! peace and countless blessings!

Love, Peter

THE MAGIC MAN

PETER OF MYSTIC MOUNTAIN

P.O. Box 1515 • Gatlinburg, TN 37738

ISBN1-878682-00-8

FOREWORD

Have you ever hoped to meet a real wizard? As a little boy or girl, did you ever make believe that you were in some deep, dark enchanted forest? Exciting, wasn't it? There you met a very wise, strange man who entertained you with his love, laughter and magic. He danced and sang with all his bird and animal friends of the forest. He was a wonderful being -- a friend to everyone and everything. Now, how would you like to make that dream come true and meet that real, living wizard?

As friends of Peter, we would like to introduce him to you. We fondly call him the "Magic Man." A friend said, "He seems to embody all the heroes of myth and legend . . . to me he was a combination of Castaneda's Don Juan and one of Tolkiens high elves."

Another friend said, "You'd almost think he was the hero of Richard Bach's book, *Illusions*. But Peter is not fiction. He is alive and real."

Who will the "Magic Man" be for you? And on what mysterious quest will he lead you? If that daring, adventuresome child within you is still alive, we invite you to meet the "Magic Man."

If you dare to travel with us, then turn this page!

INTRODUCTION

WITH PETER

INTRODUCTION
WITH PETER

Who is Peter -- the "Magic Man"?

PETER: Oh, nobody really . . . just a common old catcher of hearts. Nothing for you to be concerned about.

Peter, can I ask you to be serious?

PETER: You could probably ask me to be an airplane, but I doubt it would work.

All right Peter, my question again -- who is the "Magic Man"?

PETER: Oh well, if you insist. Ready? I am a reflection of your joy, your peace, your love. I am what you truly are, but have not yet recognized. I am all that you pretend not to be. I am your heart. I am your soul. I am your spirit. I am your happiness and your pain. I am your sorrow and your bliss . . . I am all that you are and more. I am all that you refuse to accept. I am all of you, beating in one heartbeat.

Please, since you are looking into the mirror of my eyes, see that what you have really asked is, "Who am I?" That, dear soul, is the original question of every being. And it is *only* when you know who you are, that you can dance. That you can sing. That you can celebrate!

How is it that all this "magic" -- all these miraculous events -- happens around you?

PETER: Oh, is that what you wanted to know? . . . Well . . . it's all done with mirrors. If you read "*The Magic Man*" book, it will prove it to you. I promise.

I don't quite understand what you mean?

PETER: About the mirrors?

Yes, about the mirrors.

PETER: Oh.

Will you explain what you meant by the statement, "It's all done with mirrors"?

PETER: You live in a world of a million mirrors. Each and every face is a reflection of your own.

The "magic" and the "miraculous" are only your loving eyes and your blissful heart. My dear sweet and tender friend, how, oh how, can I show you the "magic" that you are? How can I show you how "miraculous" you are? Loved one, if you clean the dust of demand from the mirror of your life, you will reflect a million suns shining at the same time.

"Magic" will dawn as a day star rising in your heart. Oh yes, my friend, it is done with mirrors, but not quite as you might expect.

(. . . long silence . . .)

Hmmm . . . No . . . that's not what I expected to hear.

PETER: I know . . .

(Peter puts his hand on my shoulder;
a tear is rolling down his cheek.
A strange, yet familiar,
sensation overcomes me.)

Peter, I feel I am dying . . . ?

PETER: Yes, I know . . . all that is not love always does . . . I'll hold your hand. Remember you wrote about it? The pool? Your experience in Florida . . .

THE MAGIC MAN

. . . I did not know Peter then, but we sat across the pool from each other every day. He drew my attention to an uncomfortable measure.

We both seemed to keep the same pool hours. I on my side, reading Jeffrey Archer and Robert Ludlum; he on his side, reading things I had never seen before.

Periodically I would go for a swim, entering the pool on my side, then swimming to the steps on the far end -- the neutral side. This went on for a few weeks. Then life, as I thought it to be, changed.

I dove into the pool one very warm day and while under water, a calling, my inner consciousness . . . God? -- I still don't know what, told me, "If you want to know who you are, if you want to fulfill your destiny, see the man."

I had no doubt as to who "the man" was and, while still under water, I swam to the ladder closest to him. Never had I swum to that ladder before; it was on *his* side!

I climbed the ladder and walked over to this man who observed my every move. He was motionless as I approached, just his eyes feeling and speaking as I had never experienced before. Looking into his eyes, and walking toward him, was like walking deeper into a tunnel. He was looking beyond the surface me. He was inviting me to go within him.

Dripping wet, I outstretched my arm and introduced

myself. He took my hand and said, "I know who you are. I am Peter. I have been waiting for you."

The birth of this lifetime. The liberation from a million frustrations and questions of purpose. I held the hand of eternity and absolutely knew it.

I sat on one side with my rock 'n' roll and my books of murder and scandal, then dove into the symbolic water of the unconscious and emerged on the other side where waited an angel of God. This angel took my hand and, as many times as I have not been worthy of such grace, he has not let go.

It is a very incredible thing to be loved.

A lot of outlandish people live in Fort Lauderdale. My wife and I had spent our first six months in Florida just getting used to them. There was the lady who had her poodles dyed to match various outfits she wore, and the guy who had a different color stretch Cadillac for every day of the week! But then, at the opposite end of the spectrum were the people living out of shopping carts and sleeping in the bushes by the beach. I suppose there was a weird sort of balance in these extremes. There was not a religious oddity or bizarre health restorative that did not have its vocal adherents, and the range of personal expression ran a gamut that truly boggled our minds and quite replaced the more conventional forms of spectator entertainments. Is it really any wonder then, that we were at least willing to *try* a psychic church?

It was billed as a "meeting" -- not a church -- but suffered from most of the latter's shortcomings. Roughly ten minutes into the opening "mini-readings" we knew we'd made a mistake.

"I sense a case of hives in . . . oh . . . August. Does that seem familiar to you?"

"No."

"Don't worry, it will come to you."

Well, somehow we hoped it wouldn't! Just to be sure, we determined to leave as soon as there was a polite break.

When the break came, we started making ours -- only to be intercepted by a new arrival. A tanned arm stuck its hand out in front of me. Blame strong social conditioning -- but I shook it.

"Hi, I'm Peter!" said the man attached to the arm.

He started talking, and, a couple of minutes into it, we knew he'd had *too* much sun! Oh, he was pleasant enough -- in fact, he was downright friendly. It was just the occasional offhand comment he'd let slip about doing things that were clearly at odds with the physical laws of the universe that tipped us off. But those eyes! There was something about those twinkling eyes . . .

Several weeks later I was walking on the beach, drinking the fresh ocean breeze for lunch, when a tanned arm stuck its hand out in front of me.

"Hi, I'm Peter -- you remem-"

"How could I forget!" I blurted before I could catch myself. He grinned, as did the raven-haired lady who had also been with him the first time we met. Maybe he's a gigolo, I thought.

"Been back to 'The Duke's' church?" he asked amiably.

"The psi-sty? No thanks! Not my cup of tea." Belatedly, I realized he was probably a regular, and my cheeks pinked.

"Yeah, not for us either -- pretty strange goings-on there!"

Boy, now there was the pot calling the kettle black, I thought! I crossed my arms and started shuffling the sand with a toe. There was a pause, and I used the time to try and calculate some graceful escape. Then he lightly clapped a friendly hand on my shoulder and said, "You know, I'll bet you're the kind of guy who straightens other people's pictures when you walk into a room."

My mind wet itself and fainted! How in the hell had he known that? *No* one knew that -- not even my wife! I never let *anyone* see me straighten their crooked pictures! His face swam out of focus and I gave him a prolonged opportunity to inspect my fillings while I fought to recover my composure.

"How the hell did you know that?" Okay, not a brilliant recovery.

He just laughed, and those eyes of his twinkled in an even *more* lively way than before.

"Oh, just a lucky guess."

"Lucky guess! Hey, how are you at guessing lottery numbers?" I was getting to feel like my old self again.

"You wanna win the lottery?" he asked incredulously.

"Well, who doesn't!" I snorted, feeling as though I'd just dispensed cosmic truth.

"Heavens, not me! Too much trouble, all that money!" He started strolling off down the beach. I stood for a moment, staring perplexedly at the spot he'd just vacated, then quickly joined him, unwilling to break the tenuous connection his strange magnetism had woven around me.

We walked to where Ann, the raven-haired lady, was daring the surf to catch her toes. He caught her hand as we went by, and gave it an affectionate squeeze. Then he turned to me and said, "Ever have any trouble with your lungs?"

My legs froze, and my fillings got another chance to tan!

"How the hell did you know that?!" Pretty original stuff, huh?

"Oh, just my lucky day, I guess." He laughed, and suddenly seemed preoccupied with a small shell he had bent to retrieve.

Ann took my arm congenially, and we kept walking. She began saying that bodily dysfunctions aren't really the problem most people think. Anything can be fixed, if you go about it in the right way. Peter caught up and reached across in front of me to hand her a quarter. She smiled -- sort of delighted-like -- and kept on explaining how disease was only pollution. We covered another hundred feet and Peter reached across in front of me and handed her another quarter. She grinned, shot me a quizzical glance and resumed. Every hundred feet or so, another quarter changed hands, and after several more, it began to dawn on me that there was no way he was finding all those coins just laying on the beach! I'd walked this stretch a hundred times and had never found anything but shell fragments. There were no pockets on his trunks, so he didn't have them stashed, either. When he handed her the next one, I couldn't keep silent any longer.

"Hey man, where are you getting all those quarters?" It seemed a pretty funny joke to them, but neither offered to explain.

By now, my lunch hour had stretched to more than two, so I left with a promise to visit them the following weekend with my wife. I turned to leave, then -- almost as an afterthought -- I asked, "By the way, where do you live?"

"Oh, right there -- number five," Ann said, indicating the building next to where I worked. Grinning, they waved and walked away. My fillings were sunburnt by the time I stopped gaping! What a strange encounter -- what odd coincidences -- what long-shot guesses -- what an amazing string of lucky coin-finds. How could all this unreasonable stuff happen in one day?

I was very late for work, but that was just as well, as I was too stunned to do any! After doodling up several sheets of paper and racing through thousands of acres of mind, I allowed I might be suffering from lightheadedness due to lack of a more substantial lunch. I also decided not to go to the beach without a hat again. You never know: too much sun can do strange things. . .

Saturday dawned clear and bright, which is more than I could say for me. For days I had wrestled with myself. Had I seen and heard correctly? How much had I imagined? When I finally explained what I thought had happened, my wife smiled and hugged me. But I'd catch her giving me long looks, searching for signs of stress and apparently hoping I hadn't become infected with the dreaded "Lauderdale lunacy." Still, the hope of finding a respite from my annual bout with bronchitis had persuaded her that it might be worth venturing one evening with crazies.

Their condo was awash with an invigorating blend of sea breeze and incense. I was surprised to feel so happy at seeing them again, and relieved to see that Mindy also seemed relaxed. This evening, they were -- well, *normal!* We laughed and talked, and I began to feel quite at ease.

We soon left for the gourmet vegetarian restaurant we had agreed to try with them. Mindy and I had eaten occasional lunches at salad bars, so we figured we could survive one dinner that low on the food chain.

While we waited for the chef to do God-knows-what to our "sprout surprises," Peter asked how I liked my line of work. I began enumerating the pros and cons as I saw them, and when I'd finished the cons had won by two lengths.

"So why don't you quit and do what you want to do?" he asked simply, as if it were the obvious solution. I didn't know whether he was being naive or rude!

"Well, you've got to do *something* for a living!" I retorted, a bit piqued.

"You do?" His face grew quizzical, and he slapped his palm on his forehead. "I *knew* there was something I was forgetting to do!" and he began to laugh uproariously.

Ann and Mindy stopped talking and helped me stare at him while the waiter delivered our "surprises." Who'd have believed you could do *that* with sprouts?

As we were leaving, Mindy tugged me to a stop and whispered excitedly in my ear, "Did you see that?"

I did a quick check around for pink elephants and UFOs. "See what?" I ventured when I'd come up empty.

"His wallet! It was empty -- well, almost empty -- it had only a couple of ones in it!" she enthused. I'd never known her to get so excited over poverty.

"Well, you may recall, he just finished piling seventeen ones on the table!" I assumed a reproving tone over her obvious lack of observation.

"No, no! That's just it! When he opened his wallet to *start* paying, there were only two bills in it!"

"Oh, come on, Mindy! If there were only two bills in his wallet, where'd he get the other fifteen -- out of thin air?" I knew I had her now, though a wispy vision of dancing quarters flashed through my mind. But she just looked triumphantly at me, her eyes aglow with wonder.

"You're not serious!" I was testing the suddenly unsteady ground. "If he were going to yank money out of the air, why not grab a twenty and take home some change? It would have been a lot less showy than all those ones!" Nothing like a little shot of practicality to steady the nerves!

"Why carry it around, when you can take out all you need whenever you want?" She turned and walked out the door with a grin so big it would have been the envy of any Cheshire cat. Curiouser and curiouser . . .

I began to think about all those quarters again. "Wow, what a way to make a living!"

"What's that?" Peter asked as he walked up beside me.

"Oh, ah, nothing, really," I stammered, embarrassed to have been caught in such larcenous musings.

"Say, you've dropped a quarter," he said, pointing to the floor by my shoe.

"But I didn't get change . . ." Then, noticing his grin, it dawned. "Well, I'll be a --"

"Watch what you wish for," he cautioned, clapping a friendly hand on my shoulder, "'cause it's bound to come true!"

I was living within my rational mind (on my way to law school, no less). Then I met Peter, and he made it his game to dispel this dead-end habit of mine.

Spiritual stuff was new to me. I had been reading a book Peter had given me, and it raised a lot of questions that challenged my most fundamental thinking.

I decided to call Peter and question him about these unfamiliar ideas -- such as mental telepathy, akashic records, etc. I dialed his number and he answered before it seemed to have had time to connect. No ring, no nothing. His first words were, "So Jaya, you have some questions for me." And he was not asking a question.

"Yes," I stammered. "How did you know it was me?"

Just laughter. Somehow all my questions seemed insignificant.

Not long after that I had some friends over for lunch on a very windy day. We decided to eat on the balcony despite the wind. During the meal, my napkin (which happened to be a paper towel) got loose and took flight. I am pollution-conscious and watched with remorse as the paper towel flew over the ten-foot hedge guarding the pool, and then into the parking lot, and then out to no-man's-land. Or so I thought.

My friends left shortly thereafter, and over an hour later I headed for work. On the way I stopped by the pool to say hello to Peter, Ann and Father Joe -- a Catholic priest from New Jersey who spent his winters in Florida. (We all were living in the same condominium building on the coast of Florida.) We stood together talking, the wind blowing at over fifteen miles an hour, when seemingly from nowhere came a paper towel which floated in the midst of the four of us. Conversation stopped as all attention focused on this phenomenon. The paper towel hovered in one spot as the wind swirled around us. I recognized the pattern on it, and suddenly realized that it was the same paper towel that had flown from my balcony!

Just as I opened my mouth to say this, the paper towel turned on its side and wrapped itself around my face. I pulled it off as though it were a live thing trying to smother me. But then again, it *was* alive, a part of the Universe that was showing me my smothered mind. I looked wide-eyed at everyone as Peter laughingly said, "I believe you lost that."

Peter's little (actually, not so little) examples of encounters with the unseen world made me stop and reevaluate my view of life and its parameters. It wasn't long after that, with the help of a few more mind-blowers, that I decided to be "irrational" the rest of my life.

Long after our move to Mystic Mountain, I remarked on how much my path had changed from the one leading to law school. Peter said, "No it hasn't; now you're learning the *real* laws of the Universe."

Instead of the "shingles" of education that are hung on an office wall, my shingles of learning were nailed on the sides of our house -- thousands of them.

So much has been written about gurus and masters and teachers. Peter cannot be put into any of these categories. With his emphasis on personal responsibility, he seems to be more like a "trainer" -- training us all for the Spiritual Olympics! He is training us all to be gold medalists, to reach the Ultimate Goal; encouraging us to be strong -- physically, emotionally, mentally and financially -- as a solid basis for true spirituality. He is training us patiently, yet persistently; lovingly, yet (most definitely!) firmly. If we stumble and falter, as we sometimes do under our heaviest weight, he is unfailingly there to support us until the day comes when that weight becomes "light" (it always does), and we move on to a more challenging arena.

What a refreshing change: here there are no rituals, no forms, no mystique. Peter would be the first to say, without hesitation, "Don't touch my *feet!*" if anyone were foolish enough to try. He is more likely to tell you to go work out!

We sat by the pool every morning when Peter and I and the others were still living in Florida. There was a contingent of about five retired folk who were ceaselessly intrigued by Peter. They sat on the other side of the pool and would talk amongst themselves about how they were going to stump him. It had become a game: they would think of a question of any variety and then challenge Peter to answer it.

This particular day the subject was geography. The group of five flocked over like chickens, and Al, their spokesman, cleared his throat and asked something like, "What is on the corner of Downy and Main Street in Nowhere Town, Indiana?" They all smiled; it was a ridiculous question and they knew it. Al had lived in Nowhere Town before retiring to Florida. They were really grasping at straws with their questions now.

Peter smiled and said matter-of-factly, "It started off as Smith's Diner but became Max's Used Car Lot in the sixties."

Al almost had the big one right there. His four friends had to drag him back to their bench. I asked Peter how he knew; had he been to Nowhere Town? He said he'd never been there and didn't even know where it was. He said he just keeps his mind clear and the answers come like subtitles across a movie screen.

Peter says that all knowledge is at our disposal when the receptor is clear to receive.

Traveling with Peter always has its surprises and never, never is it a "normal" activity.

We traveled to the house of a friend-of-a-friend in another state to help him with the restoration of a log cabin next to his home. His home was a large, well-kept house built in the mid-1800's. Our new friend greeted us at the door. We were shaking hands and saying our "How are you's" when Peter announced to our new friend, "You have a ghost in here." *Oh no,* I thought, *here we go. Not five minutes with our new friend and Peter's already off-the-wall.*

Our friend stepped back, his eyes darting between Peter and me. He turned white as a ghost himself. "How did you know?" he stammered. "I've never told anyone that. People would think I'm crazy, living by myself and all!"

Peter said that the ghost was the soul of an old woman, and that our friend had nothing to be afraid of; she was gentle and protective.

Our friend confirmed this, and added that she was the original owner of the house. Every time he tried to move any of the furniture, lamps, or pictures, she would move them all back to their original places. He had seen her ghostly form and it matched the old photos left in the house.

It was late and our friend invited us to dinner at a nearby restaurant. I was glad to be done with the ghost business, and a beer sounded good. When we walked into the restaurant, the owner, who was of a foreign nationality, took one look at Peter and came running over to us saying, "A holy man! A holy man has come to my restaurant!" *Oh shoot,* I thought. *There goes our nice quiet dinner.*

Everyone was looking at us to see the "holy man," as the owner continued to run around calling attention to us. Peter's simple, quiet manner put everyone at ease, however, and we were able to have a quiet meal after all. The rest of our time at the restaurant was made very beautiful for us. I made sure to have an extra beer, though; we were going to sleep at our new friend's house that night . . .

Cars aren't supposed to think for themselves, but I've noticed that after they've been around people for a few years, they start picking up some bad habits. They get a little lazy about starting when they're not in the mood, or if the weather doesn't strike them just right. The tires start considering holding air as optional, and radiators will all of a sudden get steamin' mad if you ask them to go up a hill on a hot day. By the time they're teenagers, cars can become downright contrary!

Fortunately, Ann's Cadillac was still preadolescent. But it had been around enough Mercedes and Porsches in Ft. Lauderdale to pick up a precocious streak of independence. So when it got contrary on the way to Tennessee, I wasn't all that surprised.

Peter lifted the hood and we stood looking at that half-acre of wires, pipes, belts and odd-looking doodads that mechanical types know by name. Being of the masculine persuasion, I felt obliged to offer opinions and advice on the off-chance that Peter wasn't a closet grease monkey. I stood there kind of shakin' my head and offering an occasional "Hmmmm" or "Uh-huh" just to get the ball rolling. Finally Peter asked, "What do you think is wrong with it?"

"Solenoid," I said. I'd heard people with grease under their fingernails say that often enough under similar circumstances.

"Maybe the battery cables are loose," Peter countered.

"No, I had a '63 Ford used to do this same exact thing -- it was the solenoid."

"Not loose cables?" Peter tried again.

"Well, I don't think so, but I've got some wrenches in the van. I'll go get them," I offered.

The van was parked on the other side of the motel, so I hiked off to get my toolbox.

When I got back five minutes later, the Cadillac was purring just as pretty-as-you-please.

"What did you do to get it going?" I asked.

"Oh, nothing really," Peter casually replied. His grin seemed a little out of place for a man who'd just had to contend with a recalcitrant car.

The toolbox was getting heavy, so I hauled it back to the van, wondering if horses and buggies had been as capricious as cars.

The next day the Cadillac gave us the silent treatment again. Peter raised the hood and we started our little ritual.

"It's the damned solenoid," I said. "It gets a little burned spot on it and sticks. It's just like my '63."

"Not battery cables?" Peter asked noncommittally.

"I'll go get the tools," I replied with resignation.

I got back with the toolbox and there she was, purrin' like a kitten again. And there was Peter, grinnin' *again.* There seemed to be some kind of pattern emerging here.

"Same thing as before, huh?" I commented.

"Yeah, it's kinda strange, isn't it?" Peter replied.

Taking the tools back, I got to thinking about some of the other "strange" things that happened so regularly whenever I was around Peter. Like the times he'd ask strangers about their hometowns or relatives by name, and they'd start into the answer as if they were old friends until it would dawn on them that he shouldn't know anything about their hometowns or relatives! Or the way people's tape recorders would suddenly go on the fritz when they'd try to record one of his evening sessions. Now, this guy bent the rules from time to time, and I was beginning to wonder if Ann's Cadillac was just an innocent bystander in this game.

The third time it happened, I decided not to say anything about the solenoid. We stood gazing across the alien-looking landscape of dusty black parts for a minute or so, and then I volunteered to go get the tools. I went around the corner of the building and leaned up against the warm brick wall to absorb the morning sun for a while. Then I returned to the purring Cadillac and my grinning friend.

"Where are the tools?" Peter asked.

"Aw, come on, Pete," I said. "You don't need tools to fix this car. You just wait till I'm out of sight!"

Just then Ann and my wife Mindy arrived. Ann asked, "Is he doing *that* again?"

"Does he do it all the time?" I inquired.

She rolled her eyes heavenward, laughed, and got into the car.

Oh great, I thought. *You mean you actually get used to this sort of thing after a while?*

Mindy's hand found mine and she said, "Do you s'pose that's why he always says, 'There's no such thing as a problem?'"

The realtors said no such piece of land existed. But Peter said it did. Who you gonna believe -- the Experts *or* an Unusual Person?

So, six of us packed our earthly goods into one of those "Rent-a-Headache" vans and left Florida's sunny beaches for the forests of the Smoky Mountains. Hey, thirteen-acre lots *can* be mislaid in any small city . . . can't they?

The van was supposed to hold six rooms of furniture. When I rented it, I figured we had maybe five rooms' worth, tops. Turned out to be more like *nine* rooms' worth when we loaded. It took four of us to close the door -- three of us squeezing in the mattresses and one pushing on the door.

Thirteen lost acres right in town, huh? I used to be such a sensible person . . .

As we crossed the border from Florida into Georgia, Gary (my copilot) spotted a Weigh Station sign. Since the bulging bus was licensed as a truck, these stops were NOT optional. So, feeling like a dinghy in a fleet of cargo ships, we pulled into line with the eighteen-wheelers.

If it weren't that these thirteen acres had to be right on the border of the Smoky Mountains National Park, maybe . . .

Got any idea how much all your furniture and clothes weigh put together? Neither did we! However, all trucks have a load limit, so as we crept onto the scale,

Gary and I each took a deep breath, hoping to buoy up our overstuffed van.

It didn't work. The loudspeakers barked "Pull over!" in a decidedly unamused tone. Sheepishly, feeling somehow disgraced, we pulled over to await the pronouncement of whatever penalty Georgia saw fit to impose upon people with overweight furniture.

When it came right down to it, what did Gatlinburg have to offer that Ft. Lauderdale didn't?

The prosecutor turned out to be a drill sergeant in a Smoky Bear hat who no doubt had been Genghis Khan in a former life. He rapped the swollen ribs of our van with his knuckles and said, "What you boys truckin' in heah?"

Now between Gary and me, we had more hair than an entire Marine battalion put together. I could see my expression grow slightly apprehensive in the drill sergeant's mirrored sunglasses.

"You aren't haulin' no contraband organic materials are you?"

I could only assume he meant marijuana, and I remembered the stories I'd heard in Florida about vehicles being completely dismantled by Feds in search of illicit drugs. My mind flooded with images of all our clothes and furniture spread out across acres of blacktop amidst fenders, wheels, door panels and radio knobs.

Without thinking, I said, "There goes my deposit."

"What's that?!!!" he barked.

I said, "No sir, not us."

Casually, he put one hand on his hip by his holster and said, "No house plants or fruit?"

"House plants? Fruit?" Neither Gary nor I were feeling particularly original just then. I'm afraid we started to laugh.

"Let's open her up and have a look inside, boys!" The drill sergeant was growing less amused by the moment.

I was reaching for the door handle when I saw the padlock I'd snapped on in Florida. *Hey, you never know -- someone might want overweight furniture . . .*

I looked on my keyring -- no. I slapped my pockets -- no. I turned them inside out -- no. Gary slapped his pockets and turned them inside out -- no.

The drill sergeant began tapping his foot in the most annoying way. I tugged on the offending padlock -- no. Just as I started off to see if Mindy had the key I ran into Peter coming around the side of the van. With his long blond hair and beard, and his deep mahogany tan, he looked more like a surfer than an upstanding citizen.

No, Pete, not now! I thought. *The sarge is about to shoot the lock off already!* But Peter had rounded the corner, so I scrambled back, hoping the three of us might be able to wrestle the drill sergeant down if things went from bad to worse. *God, I'm really beginning to miss Florida.*

Peter, with a huge beaming smile, was asking Mirror-Eyes what the problem was.

"I can't find the damned padlock key," I volunteered.

Peter reached down, pulled open the padlock and removed it.

"Well, that's no problem," he said.

The drill sergeant backed off a couple paces. Gary and I struggled as hard to close our gaping mouths as we did to push that roll-up van door into furniture-occupied territory.

Well, maybe Gatlinburg has some promise after all . . .

Maybe it was the awful ripping and crunching sounds the door was making in its attempt to force passage through our furnishings -- or maybe it was the unusual person who opened padlocks with his bare hands -- I don't know. The drill sergeant, however, suddenly developed a consuming interest in being elsewhere! He curtly dismissed us and marched off to accost less dangerous smugglers.

We turned to Peter: "How did you *do* that?!?"

He smiled and pulled up a sleeve. "See, nothing up here."

Oh, and you can imagine how surprised the realtors were to find a "lost" thirteen-acre lot with the National Park bordering three *sides!*

There were six of us in the Cadillac as it groaned its way up the steep, twisting road of a mountainside residential area in Tennessee. We were headed for "The Barn," a fine example of Neo-Stone Age architecture that a local entrepreneur had called a "rental chalet" *without* laughing right out loud! It was our temporary home while we waited for the thirteen-acre "lost continent of Mystic Mountain" to be *re*discovered.

It was a hot summer's day as six friends, lost in their own thoughts, sloshed back and forth in the Cadillac as it bravely battled gravity up the steep curves of a snaky road we'd all come to know so well. And then it was gone! In the blink of an eye, we were miles away on another road that led to a condo we had rented during our first week in town!

"Hey!" I blurted, "What are we doing here?"

"How did we get here?" Ann inquired more appropriately.

Mindy hummed the theme from *The Twilight Zone,* and Peter just laughed.

The Cadillac lurched into another hard right, and we were back!

"Where do you think you are?" Peter asked.

"Well, now we're back here!" Gary said.

"But we weren't a second ago!" I added defensively. "We were up on Campbell Lead by the Highlands!"

That met with a chorus of "yeahs" and "rights," but

you'd have thought we were all great comedians the way it set Peter off!

It was becoming abundantly clear to all of us that simultaneous mass insanity was *not* to blame for our momentary group translocation.

"How did you *do* that?" Gary asked.

"It's all done with mirrors," Peter giggled.

Five pairs of bulging eyes looked warily at one another while each of us wrestled with the all-consuming question of whether we should wait to pack or just run yelling and screaming down the hill!

Peter had gathered a few people of unique talents and abilities to move to Tennessee and help build the house and Center on Mystic Mountain. We lay dormant and restless for many months while negotiations for land, etc. were in progress. The restlessness of ambitious people can build quite rapidly. When we confronted Peter about things, he said, "Whatever needs to be done to make you feel useless will be done." And that was that! And that was extremely effective.

The nothing-to-do syndrome got old quickly, however, especially when it rained every day for three months. Cooped up inside, we wondered if Peter were just plain crazy. Every morning we would wake up to rain and wonder what to do to keep from going stir-crazy and how to quell the powerful feeling of cabin fever. Peter would come down every morning with his "never say die" attitude, ready to set the world on fire. Amidst our failing hopes, Peter would affirm time and time again, "We are the miracle-working power in everything we desire to have done." Have you ever wanted to smash a skipping record?

But the miraculous kept our minds at bay and our hearts alive. Like the time our refrigerator quit running one Saturday evening. Peter sought out all the appropriate people to repair it, but no one would respond. He made one last call, getting the same no-help response. Then he lifted his arms in the air, clapped his hands and said, "I guess I will have to fix it" . . . and the refrigerator started running.

Oh, there were many miraculous happenings daily around Peter. But it was his vision, hope and love that carried us all.

Things really got low when the owner of the house we were renting called to say he wanted us to move out immediately. We were all unpleasantly surprised, except for you-know-who! He was pleasantly excited by this challenge.

A wave of anxiety ran through us. Peter smiled and went up to his room. (He had no phone upstairs for communicating with anyone outside the house.) He came back downstairs a few hours later with a scheming smile and walked directly to the phone, which rang once before he got there. He answered, "Hello, Mr. Little" . . . the man from whom we were renting.

Mr. Little had called back to say that he had changed his mind and would like us to stay as long as we pleased, and that he was interested in the possibility of helping us with our project. Peter laughed and laughed at us. But in the midst of his laughter, he stopped and lowered his eyes of knowing and love, and asked, "When are you going to release your doubts?" Then he continued his merry laughter unhindered.

Peter was always there to point out (or burst) the illusions we were creating -- such as the night our small group felt we had cause for concern because we thought we were being watched. The tension mounted and we were all on guard. One of us heard footsteps outside, and we were buzzing like a disturbed bee hive. Peter, sensing the commotion, came a-hoppin' and a-skippin' down the stairs saying that the "Descended Master Gumby" had come to give us a blessing. He ran outside to pay his respects. We were all left standing there, embarrassed at our anxiety.

We finally got exactly the land we wanted, and the rain stopped just as we started building. We were all happy and working hard again. The lessons we learned in that rental house (classroom)! It was our first real experience of being with Peter all day, every day. During those times of so many changing emotions, our captain always stayed calm in his vision with his sights on his goal. He was always happy and experiencing life anew, always laughing. It was irritating. It was wonderful. It was a blessing -- because when it was all over, we truly knew that peace from within was possible. Our friend was, and is, unwavering.

The way Peter approaches life is a constant inspiration and example of faith and trust. Clearing our property for the building site on Mystic Mountain proved to be a wonderful opportunity for Peter to help us see more clearly the results of total trust in the Divine Plan.

We were cutting to clear the way for electric lines to the Center. The largest of the trees we had cut got caught in the "Y" of another. This always creates a touchy and dangerous situation. We tried our come-along till all the cables were broken. We tried every means at our disposal, but the tree didn't budge an inch. We decided to work further down the hillside.

Hal and Ann were saying that maybe, just maybe, we could get some divine help on this one. It was very hot and we were all a bit edgy -- except for Captain Optimism.

Peter sailed down the mountain to start the process again. When we were all out of reach of our hung-up tree -- it fell! We couldn't believe it! We had spent two hours trying to do that.

Peter's laughter resounded across the mountainside. We were all suddenly full of energy and happy again, feeling quite in grace. Peter said, "Be aware of this universal truth displayed for you today: do all you can, and divine energy will always do the rest; but first, you must do all you can."

Another time during the clearing, a large branch with a three-inch diameter broke loose and was falling straight down -- perfectly positioned to give Peter a good crack over the head. A few feet above his head, the branch broke in two and fell to each side of him. We questioned him about such good fortune. He said it was "divine insurance" and that it was the best policy he'd ever had.

We were getting the message, and the miraculous examples kept coming and coming.

Peter, Gary and I threw a rope around a large limb that was in the way of the electric lines. Instead of the whole tree, we attempted to remove only the hindering branch. It was large and stubborn. We pulled and yanked and pulled and yanked, each time getting more daring and closer to being directly under the branch itself. Our strategy wasn't brilliant, but we were not going to lose the challenge!

Crack!! I dove for my life one way, Gary dove for his the other. Peter had no concern for his -- he just stood there. I looked up upon hearing Captain Optimism's song of laughter. Both arms were raised up in the air and the huge branch was suspended four feet above his head by a mere briar vine. The vine was at the exact balancing point of the limb, holding it suspended like a mobile. "About that divine insurance," I asked him, "who's your agent?"

That year the yellow jackets were very prolific and we had our run-ins with them. Peter, Hal and I were cutting-in the driveway when I pulled up an old log and de-roofed a large nest. Hal and I took off running with the little buggers all over us. Thanks to some quick thinking by the others who were there, we didn't get stung too many times. Peter was the closest to the nest when I pulled up the log; he stood there like a child in awe, looking at all the bees. He was so excited -- he had never seen so many bees before! Not a one even landed on him.

Peter's demonstrations of faith were numerous back then, but it was also a time when we needed all we could get. Peter was and is a constant reminder that "God watches over even the sparrows in the sky."

I met Peter one sunny afternoon in the summer. I had walked up the road through some woods at the edge of town. I saw him on the roof of his house, perched at treetop level like a bird preparing for flight. He came down, or, rather, he appeared to fly down, to greet me. He looked like a blond version of the pictures of Jesus -- long, pale-golden hair and beard, and a face so open that I could see the joy dancing from his bright blue eyes. "Hello," he said with a warmth that encircled me just before his hug. I found myself chasing glimpses of memories that were as elusive as butterflies floating through a meadow. In his face that day, the glimpse I caught was a reminder of a long-forgotten peace.

In my early days with Peter, I wanted to be on the "fast track." I wanted quick spiritual results -- like fast-food and instant credit. Peter, as a living example, has taught me to value and be content with things accomplished "one step at a time."

"Will you work on me?" I asked, the question popping out one afternoon as we were putting shingles on the house. The desire to transform myself with Peter's help had been growing, and had prompted this request. I knew Peter loved to joke, especially when he was "working on you." I had heard many funny stories of the little traps he would set to trip the ego and bring awareness. I knew my sense of humor would need to serve me well in this quest. He seemed to measure me as he looked directly into my eyes and said, "Do you know what you ask?" "Yes," I answered quickly, with more faith than knowing. I came to know that it is a loving hammer with which he chisels, and that each experience of "letting go" brings more laughter and more light.

While building Mystic Mountain, our friend Roy was getting pretty shaken by the unusual events going on. One particular day the weather was foul, and the power kept going out. Roy prided himself on his electrical skills and would, with each power failure, run to our utility pole to check on the breakers, etc. Each time he would come back dejected because he couldn't find the answer to the problem. Roy would stoically climb the ladder to the deck and shrug his shoulders.

Then Peter would say, "I'll take care of it," and descend the ladder just enough for his head to get out of sight. Then he'd pop back up -- not even a second out of sight -- and yell, "Okay, give it a try." Of course, to everyone's astonishment, the power would come on.

This happened three times during the course of the morning: Roy running down to the pole only to come back despondent; Peter popping out of sight for a blink, then yelling, "Okay, give it a try." The fourth time the power went out, everyone yelled, "Roy!" By this time Roy had had enough. He couldn't figure it out. He yelled back, "Just shove your damn cords in Peter's pocket!"

The weather was amazingly cooperative while we were building. One day, it was raining everywhere except over us. Roy had started to pick up his tools a few times because rain was within 100 yards of the house on all sides. Each time, Peter asked him where he was going. Roy responded that it was raining all around us and that we might as well go home. Peter countered with, "It will not rain on us; let's continue working." Roy hesitated but started working again.

This happened a few times that morning and every time Peter said, "Roy, it is not going to rain on us, keep working." After about the fourth time, Roy started pacing the deck like a man about to lose it. He marched to one side where it was raining, then to the other side where it was raining. He crossed to the third side and saw rain, and then, hopelessly, to the fourth, where he also saw rain. Rain surrounding us on all sides, but not a drop on us.

Peter and I watched this perplexed young man with great amusement. Roy just couldn't accept what was happening. What he *could* grasp, he didn't like, and he came over to us, almost mad at the whole thing. "All right," he demanded, "where's the sunshine, Mister Weatherman?"

Peter raised his arm and pointed to the sky above. The clouds thinned and spread enough for a stream of sunshine to fall upon us. Roy, in a fit of nervousness, started singing, "Blue skies, nothing but blue skies." I said, "Pretty neat stuff, huh?" He replied that his rational mind was trying to keep cool over it all, but that he was starting to become very concerned.

After we finished building, a year went by with no word from Roy until one afternoon when he drove up with a few of his friends. He had brought them to see "the magic man who fixes things without doing anything and who controls the weather."

I had been with Peter for more than a year constructing the house and Center in Tennessee. I planned a vacation to the beach, looking forward to a little extra space. Peter's incredible dynamic energy can be consuming, and his all-knowingness can be nerve-wracking. I thought that getting away from his presence alone would be a vacation. WRONG!

My traveling companion asked me about Peter as we were driving toward the beach. The conversation became very sincere and emotional. I felt an overwhelming appreciation for the love and help Peter gives so freely. Tears started coming down my cheeks, and I drifted off into my own world as I felt Peter's presence right there with me. My friend pulled off the road, and we sat there for a few minutes until I felt the presence leave. I started to wonder why my friend had pulled off the road; I looked over at her only to find that she had tears flowing down her cheeks also. She looked at me with such innocence and said, "I think Peter was here." Then she broke into a beautiful, radiant smile. Yes, Peter had been there! I thought he had just been in my world, but he had been in my friend's too.

I was on vacation to get away from him, yet it seemed he was following me! My friend and I found a nice spot on the beach to set up camp. I was lying down, drifting off to sleep, when a dog came right up and startled me with its sniffing nose. Its nose touched my cheek, and I looked up, wide-eyed, trying to get my bearings. I looked at the dog and it looked at me. We were transfixed for only a second, though it seemed a day could have gone by. I shook my head, breaking that strange here-now experience, and wondered what had transpired. Then the dog's master called for it, and off it ran.

I didn't think much about the whole thing until that night. I called home and the first thing Peter said was, "Did you see me today?" *Well,* I thought, *I felt him, but I didn't see him in the car.* I was silent for a moment and he said, "I was the dog on the beach!" He laughed, full of the joy of his game.

I thought, *if my whole vacation is going to be like this, I might as well go home.* There is no getting away from Peter's love!

I loved reading *Miracle of Love* by Ram Dass. Especially enjoyable was the relationship between the Master and Dada. I had been living with Peter for a while and could relate to the "abuse."

As we worked at building the house on Mystic Mountain, Peter would create situations in which I would get very frustrated and mad at him (or at myself -- depending on how you look at it); situations where he would say one thing, then do another. He would criticize my work when there was nothing wrong with it. He would want to do things the hard or long way just to see how I reacted. I hated it and loved it. It was a mess. It was frustrating. How many times I cursed him under my breath and thought him crazy! But I was there by my own choice, and I figured I was none the worse for it. And always, just as I would reach my breaking point, Peter would say, "What's the matter, Dada?" Even in my bleakest moments (when I had mentally packed my bags), whenever he said that, I couldn't help but smile and laugh at myself as the warmth of his love spread through me.

Lessons are so hard when you are feeling negative emotions. When Peter called me "Dada," as he did many times, the illusions I had set up would break under his loving hammer. The house we built came out wonderfully, and by the time we had finished it a few years later, I was doing pretty well too.

My question was basically simple,
"Why did he share his soul so totally with me?"
His heart so completely open
pouring a Divine Elixir into mine.
His eyes revealing the allness of himself
gazing into mine, revealing my allness to me.
His mind peering gingerly into the mind of my own,
accepting me as I am.
Being gentle like a lamb,
his balance so perfect,
his strength so real
that he could even be the lion that he is.
This lion jumping to action
making the love so real.
His sharing of himself,
his tears, dear God, his tears,
his eyes
again, his eyes.
He looked at me
into me
through me
in order to be *with* me.
He taught me.
He healed me.
He spoke with me
Though not always sharing words at this time.
He declared my specialness
and I balked, "Of course, for aren't we all?"

He loved me through words of sincerity
offering love in the way I could understand.
"Why did he share his soul so totally with me?"
"Love, Life, the Moment," I answer
"What else is there?" you say . . .
He says.

I awoke to the sound of Peter making a fire. We meditated together every morning and this sound was my cue that it was "that time" again. But when I looked at my clock, it read 2 a.m. The normal time for our meditation was around 6 a.m. Sleepily, I went down and sat next to him.

I hesitated to break his concentration, but I whispered, "What are you doing? It's 2 a.m." Peter said, "Oh," then got up and left. I continued to sit for over an hour, waiting for him to come back. He did not come back. I went to get more sleep.

Six a.m. came around and I heard Peter again making a fire. I decided to ignore the whole thing this time, but I heard "J--a--y--a" coming from downstairs. So I got up to sit with him. I asked him where he had gone, leaving me sitting there in the middle of the night. He said he had gone back to bed, and that "only crazy people meditate at 2 a.m."

Funny, I had been thinking the same thing myself.

Peter has a very structured outline for me -- it is to prevent me from creating a structured outline. I tend to regiment things and overdo surface disciplines, such as when I thought I would start getting up at 3 a.m. to meditate. Peter said he didn't think this to be a good idea, but to do what made me happy. I set my clock anyway: 3 a.m. I awoke late the next morning to a stopped clock that never worked again. I told Peter and he said, "That proves it's not a good idea."

It still sounded like a good idea to me, though. I had read that this was what high spiritual beings do, and I was determined to be one. I still had my clock/radio. I set it: 3 a.m. I awoke late the next morning to a stopped clock. It was never to work again. This hurt; the clock had a lot of sentimental value. I had had it over fifteen years. I told Peter of the fate of the clock/radio and told him he owed me one. Nonetheless, I said, I got the message. He said, "Good."

Ah, but I still had my watch! A few weeks later I tried again. My watch didn't have an alarm, so I woke up every couple of hours so as not to miss 3 a.m. -- the magic hour! At midnight that night, my Timex of nine years, my Timex that never stops ticking, stopped ticking . . . never to work again. When I saw Peter the next morning, he was happy as usual and bid me a good morning. I bid him a, "You owe me three!"

After that I had little choice but to awaken when I naturally awakened, and to sleep when I fell asleep. I owned nothing that told time. This was actually a liberating and transforming process for me. It was wonderful!

Mystic Mountain is, quite simply, my favorite place to be. I love everything about it -- and everything is something of a mystery there.

How is it that *there,* we get to see perhaps the only bear in the whole Bear Kingdom with a white circle over his heart?

Why is it that the fire crackles and pops when Peter makes a point?

Listen! The wind chimes are ringing. But where is the wind?

And how come the weather happens just right?

The bees make more honey, the tomato vines bend over with their gifts.

And the people? Hmmm, they get to be Divine.

There are spots on the planet where the vortex of energy swirls like the fastest whirlwind -- so fast that it appears to be still.

It is so subtle, and as *we* get more so, we just feel it more.

Every mandala has a center -- this is one of those,

Where God's love radiates out, healing all it touches -- touching all . . .

And it seems that a man in beat-up tennis shoes has something to do with it . . .

I don't know how the funds materialized for the airfare, for I was totally depleted -- physically and emotionally, as well as financially -- but they somehow did, and with a mixture of excitement and trepidation, I was finally on my way to the Mountain for the first time.

My friend Jaya met me at the airport and, as we drove for an hour to our destination, many thoughts and feelings ran through me -- and questions! I remember asking Jaya at least a hundred questions. Finally, as we drove up the gravel road, the house came into view. I hadn't known what to expect, but the first glimpse of the house told me my visit was going to be really something. Awe and anticipation welled up within me. "You haven't seen anything yet!" Jaya said with a laugh. We entered the house -- so white, so light, so peaceful and beautiful . . . so very beautiful. It was evening, and there were candles, soft lighting, incense, plants and flowers. I felt like I had somehow landed in Shamballah.

Peter bounded up the stairs and wrapped my torn body, mind and spirit in his arms. The first of countless hugs. His fragrance then, as now, was delightful. His smile, his warmth, his luminosity, put me at ease. All my questions were answered in that one hug. At last, oh God!, at long, long last, I had come home.

It takes courage, or craziness (probably both!), to keep knocking at that door. Every contact with Peter is totally fresh and unique. There is no past, and there is no future. How he responded to me yesterday does not exist today, and today's contact is not going to set a pattern for tomorrow. There is no time continuum, no habitual relating. This can be very challenging!

I had climbed the mountain for half an hour, seeing only squirrels searching under snow-covered leaves, and large clumps of snow dropping from sun-warmed branches. Thoughts raced through my mind about the future, and about why I wasn't feeling the experience of closeness from living with a spiritual teacher that many of the others seemed to be feeling with Peter.

My answer came from the inner voice that has guided me through many unexplainable experiences. It clearly stated, "I am with you always."

The profundity of that simple statement halted my climb and simultaneously revealed the presence of three fawns watching me from less than 100 feet away. I later realized that they were the same fawns who seemed to follow Peter wherever he went in the woods. Since then I have often wondered if I would have seen him with them if I had looked hard enough.

Peter is surrounded by beauty. The house he designed and built sits on the Mountain like an exotic oriental ship, waiting to set sail. It is a reflection of Peter, from the solid foundation to the many large light-filled windows; from the towering fireplace to the soaring roof peaks. Surrounding the house, trees and flowers abound -- everything is lush and fertile. A casual passerby might wonder if they had stumbled upon the original Garden of Eden were they to glimpse the abundance and variety of wildlife around the house. It seems as if all the birds from the whole mountain gather there to sing their songs of love and life. The deer graze in a relaxed and contented way; black bears (which are rarely seen in surrounding areas) roam around the house like unique guard dogs, bringing their cubs at an early age to bask in this environment. All the animals of the forest come -- foxes, opossum, raccoons, even the wild boar. Why do they come? They come because, like us, they feel totally safe and loved. Peter strokes the deer as we might stroke a pet cat, and he plays with the bears as we might with a frisky puppy!

It's uncanny how Peter is always there supporting and loving us at just the right times. He seems to know everything about us . . . our highs and our lows. Sometimes there are times when a person just needs to be loved, no questions asked. The power of Peter's love instantly casts away the heaviest depression or despondency.

One day I had been feeling "The Void" all day. By evening, the feeling was very intense . . . one of empty aloneness. Just as I felt that all was going to cave in, Peter called to say he had felt me "pulling at his heart strings." He had called just to tell me, "I am here to fill the void." I felt so totally loved and cared for; he had called at exactly the right time. By the following day, the "Miracle of Existence" again permeated my being.

Two of my friends have had similar experiences:

"It was the end of a discouraging day, and I arrived home thoroughly depressed. Nothing seemed to be going well, and I felt myself sinking into a black well of despair. 'Life is the pits,' I thought. 'No one cares. What's the use?' Then I noticed my answering machine blinking, indicating that someone had called. I pushed the button and heard, 'Hello. This is Peter. Just wanted to say that I love you.' And the sun came out. Peter was there again, just when I needed his loving grace."

"It was a gray dark day with lots of heavy clouds, and I was very depressed. I decided to stay home instead of going to the Mountain for the Sunday meditation. The following day I arrived home from school and found a letter from Peter in my mailbox. The letter said that they had missed me Sunday and that 'Even if the rains come, it's all for the flowers' growth. Love, Peter.'

He had to have mailed it Saturday for the letter to arrive on Monday, but I didn't even know I wasn't going to meditation until that Sunday! The miracle of the timing, as well as the caring message, instantly warmed my heart again to the joy of life."

My dear friend Diana lay dying, and although intellectually my mind was saying, "There's no such thing as death. She'll be free for new adventures," my heart was full of pain. I didn't want to let her go.

I left her bedside and walked back toward town to the post office, hoping that the walk would help to quiet my inner turmoil. I found a note from Peter in my box, offering simple words of encouragement and love. As I read them, I felt a sensation of peace wash over me. Suddenly I was all right, at peace with myself and with the fact that Diana had chosen to leave.

At 7:00 that night I received a call from Diana's closest friend telling me that Diana had died about two hours earlier . . . just at the time I had been reading Peter's note and feeling the peace wash through me, and, I realized, through Diana too.

Peter is always there to tend my deepest hurts. The presence of his love has helped me deal with and heal some deep emotional wounds. His love is as perfect as his timing.

Even a routine outing to the local gym can become extraordinary with Peter. It started while we were doing bench presses. Peter was a bit quieter than usual as we progressed to our heaviest set with maximum weight. It was Peter's turn and we put on the weight he normally used for his maximum of three lifts. He sat quietly, and slowly looked around the gym to see if anyone were watching. Nobody was paying any attention to us. He lay down and did his three lifts with a great deal of struggle. I reached for the bar to set it on the rack, when Peter said "Wait." He picked up his head slightly to confirm that no one was looking, then proceeded to do ten more lifts with the same weight, effortlessly, without the slightest sign of struggle. He had to put the bar back on the rack himself; I was in a state of frozen shock. He got up, looked at me with a smile and said, "Even you can do that. All the power of the Universe is within you. When you know and believe that it is."

Believing that all power is within *him* was easy. Knowing that all power is within *me* -- that would take some work, as was evidenced by my next lift.

As we proceeded to our next exercise, the son of the gym owner came in with the aid of a crutch. Earlier that day he had dropped a heavy weight on his foot and fractured it. His mother and father were in the gym as well, giving instructions to those working out. The boy loved Peter and came over when he spotted us. Peter asked what had happened, then knelt down and held the boy's swollen and bruised foot. His parents rushed over immediately; they had been suspicious of Peter from the start and obviously didn't want him to influence the boy. Seconds later, the boy let out a gasp and said he felt something strange happening to his foot. Peter kept holding it and telling him that it was going to be fine. The boy was excitedly telling his parents that the swelling was going down and that he felt a warm tingling in his foot where Peter was holding it. The parents' disapproval grew; their frowns etched deeply into their stony faces. Within a few minutes, the swelling and discoloration were totally gone. The boy was hopping on the foot to show everyone he had been healed. It was too much for the parents, however. They marched themselves and the boy out the door, plotting Peter's excommunication from the gym. The parents never said a word or even smiled at their son's healing. The boy's love was "thank you" enough.

I don't know if I was tired from the exercise or from assimilating all that had just happened, but I was ready to go and didn't even bother to put on my shoes. Peter politely suggested that I put them on. He warned me only once: he usually will only once! When I stepped off the curb, I got what felt like an electric shock as I stepped on a splinter that sank straight up into my heel. As I let out a yelp, Peter walked by mumbling something about no one listening to him.

There haven't been any workouts like that in a while. But one doesn't need many to understand that there is physical, healing and knowing power beyond our dreams.

A visiting friend was fearful of needing an operation to remove a tumor. She talked with Peter about it and came to one of his evening meditations. During the meeting, Peter told us about a vision he had received of a bear with a white circle on its chest. He said that the morning after his vision, the bear with the circle had appeared at the Mountain along with two other bears. Peter explained that the bear was sacred to the Native Americans and that they would consider a visit from one to be a great blessing: an omen foretelling good fortune for the tribe.

Immediately after the evening meditation the bears came to the upstairs deck. We all watched as Peter played with them and fed them. We noticed that when the bear with the white circle sat, the circle formed into a perfect heart!

My friend was overjoyed to have seen the bears for she was scheduled to leave the next day. Before she left, Peter told her she did not need to have a tumor and that it would be there only if she wanted it.

A few weeks later my friend called to tell me that the operation was no longer necessary because the tumor had become very small. She asked about the bear with the white circle. I told her Peter had named him "Light Heart" and that he had been a healing omen.

When I first heard of Peter and Mystic Mountain through a friend, I was skeptical. It was some time after my friend obtained tapes of Peter's talks that I listened to them. The truth that I heard on those tapes, and the impact that that awareness of the truth had on my life, were undeniable. But I was still wary. I wrote to Peter asking to attend one of his weekend seminars and was invited. What I experienced at Mystic Mountain that March was not earthshaking, but rather a gentle plucking of my heartstrings. This has continued to be my experience with Peter. The truth that I found there was not of the head but of the heart. That truth is love. It is that love that inspired my life course to change and directed me closer to Peter, the wellspring of love.

Late one summer's day, when my fragile little world seemed to be collapsing around me like a house of cards, I sent a cry from the depths of my heart to the Universe: "There has to be more than this, Lord! What is my purpose in life?"

About a month later, as my plans for a long-awaited visit home were taking shape, I received a call from my beloved sister Mindy and her husband Hal. They invited me to join them for a seminar with Peter at Mystic Mountain. Without a moment's hesitation, I answered "Yes!" Later I wondered why I had been so sure.

That first seminar with Peter was so intense for me. Part of me wanted to run from that much love and light, while the other part wanted to dissolve into it. The battle raged within until the third morning when I decided to be completely open to all that I was learning and feeling. Then the magic happened! An immense feeling of joy bubbled up inside of me, and I knew why every cell of my body had said, "Yes," even when my mind had still been questioning.

The town was empty, and as quiet as the moonlight on the softly falling snow. My friend and I walked in this luminous landscape, arguing as we went. My words of smoke-red anger were in sharp contrast to the white peace of the snow and ice.

I was glad we were alone with no one else to see my angered state. I attempted to regain my composure before returning home to children and company, determined to keep this argument to myself.

At that time I had only known Peter a few months. I was just beginning, with his help, to understand the destructiveness of anger. I had formerly encouraged my fiery nature, confusing anger with power and refusing to recognize anger as an addictive habit. Here I was, jumping on the see-saw of anger and succumbing to its stimulation, while failing to recognize the inevitable painful fall to earth when that see-saw crashed.

On arriving home, my company greeted us at the door with a message from Peter; he had called to say that my anger had disturbed him while he was taking a shower!

I will never forget the shock. I felt as though I were standing in a spotlight, totally exposed. Peter could not have known about the argument, unless, of course, there was nothing that was unknown to him. Over the years I have found this to be the case -- nothing can be hidden; Peter always "knows."

As Peter was showing me this miracle of light, allowing me to see and accept myself, I felt a spiritual longing to be free of anger and fear. I perceived this longing as a spirit which, like a plant, was turning to the light.

I reaffirmed my decision to give my fiery nature to the flames of honesty and surrender. Since then, Peter has been the shining light on my path to the mountaintop.

Years before I met Peter, there was a period in my life when I was experiencing a great loss. I felt all alone -- crying -- the whole melodrama. I remember crying out for comfort saying, "Oh Baba! Oh Jesus!"

During the course of one of his seminars Peter said, "'Oh Baba, Oh Jesus!' How are they going to help you?"

Well, the old computer couldn't reason that one! How had he known? That must have been for someone else, right? But, no, he was looking right at me as he spoke.

He did this to me again on another occasion. I had been contemplating making a trip to India and perhaps including a visit to see Sai Baba. I had not yet told anyone about my plans.

It was Christmastime at the Mountain; we were all unwrapping Christmas gifts, and I was watching Peter open his. Suddenly, he looked in my direction and said, "Sai Baba, Sai Baba, Sai Baba!" -- then continued to unwrap his gifts.

I always loved to fly, even though I experienced great pain in my ears whenever I did so. I was living in Alaska when I first met Peter, which meant I had to fly quite a bit to attend my first few seminars in Tennessee.

The second seminar I went to had been intense, and I felt that everything within me needed work. I was by no means at peace when I left the Mountain for the airport that morning.

While we were driving to the airport, Phyllis -- a new, yet somehow old, friend -- decided to play a tape with a mantra on it. As I boarded the plane the chant stayed with me, and, as I sat in my seat, it began to fill me from head to toe, creating a shimmering in the air around me and through me. Just as the plane began to lift off the ground, the beloved face of Peter flashed in my mind's eye so vividly that I felt he were there! My head cleared, my ears became free of pressure and pain, and I felt totally at peace. The rest of my trip was pain-free . . . the first in all my years of flying.

My son Jason had had trouble with his ears since birth. As an infant he had recurring ear infections because neither ear drained fluid properly. At six months he had his first surgery: small tubes were placed in each ear to open a path through his ear canal to allow the fluid to drain. The doctors said that the operation was necessary because his eardrums could burst if the fluid continued to build.

Jason's tubes would stay in place approximately a year before they would fall out on their own. As the tubes were too tiny to notice, their absence would be indicated by the return of Jason's earaches and infections. The doctor would then inform us that Jason needed tubes once more. So every year, once a year, Jason underwent surgery though, thankfully, it took only a few minutes and just a light anesthetic was necessary.

This condition continued until Jason was thirteen. Only once during this period was more extensive surgery required to repair a punctured eardrum. He had suffered severe pain in this operation and now the doctors were telling us he needed to have his eardrum repaired again. I, his mother, felt desperate.

My sister had been prodding me to take Jason to see Peter at Mystic Mountain. Finally, I did! We arrived there one evening for our appointment. Peter talked with Jason and used iridology (a way of determining one's state of health by observing the patterns in the iris of the eyes). Finally, he ran his hands around Jason's head and ears without touching him. That's all that happened.

The doctor's appointment and the appointment at Mystic Mountain took place within about a ten-day period. A few days later, we returned to the doctor for Jason's final checkup before he entered the hospital for surgery.

The doctor came in to see Jason, checked his ears, and immediately left the room. He did this several times and never uttered a word. Both Jason and I sat there in quiet anticipation, nervously awaiting the verdict. The nurse came in and took Jason to have an audiogram, then returned him to the room.

When the doctor finally returned, he seemed amazed. He said, "I can't believe this. His ear is totally healed. He doesn't need surgery!"

Jason and I were amazed, too. Although we had been told that a healing took place at Mystic Mountain the night we saw Peter, I don't think we really believed it!

No matter what medication Jason had taken in the past, nothing had ever helped him except the tubes in both ears. We had certainly expected, since he not only had had an ear infection but a punctured eardrum, that he stood no chance of recovery without surgery.

Jason and I left the doctor's office elated and totally astonished that his ear was healed. We didn't tell the doctor of Jason's experience at Mystic Mountain because we knew he wouldn't believe it -- but we did!

Jason was sixteen in April of 1989. He hasn't had ear surgery since seeing Peter (almost three years have passed). He has had several checkups, only to be informed that everything is fine and that he must have outgrown his ear problems. Each time, Jason and I look at each other and smile. *We know* what really happened -- a miracle, Jason's miracle.

Love knows all.

It's a wonderful thing to think that someone knows everything about you. Especially someone like Peter who shares and gives so much. It's a wonderful thing -- thinking about it, I mean -- but actually *being* around someone who knows your deepest secrets is another! Peter will often make reference to your personal experiences -- the ones only you yourself know, or so you think.

One night I jumped awake, startled, because I thought, or dreamed, that I had fallen asleep and left my meditation candle burning. It was out, so I went back to sleep. The next day when several of us were talking, Peter started laughing and said, "That reminds me of Jaya last night."

Everyone was inquisitive, wanting to hear more. I had no idea to what he was referring, and my bewildered expression only seemed to spur him on. Peter related how I had jumped out of bed in the middle of the night, thinking my meditation candle was burning. He felt that to be very funny. What he thought even funnier was my astounded face -- I had been sleeping in my own room with the door closed!

It can be very difficult getting used to the idea that someone actually knows things he shouldn't!

One evening when we were having a silent moment of appreciation before eating, I was inwardly repeating,

"Peace, peace, peace" to myself. When the silent period was over, Peter asked, "Who's saying 'Peace, peace, peace'?" I said I was. He said, "Not so loudly next time!"

Episodes like these make one go deep within and muster up a lot of self-acceptance. Peter's love makes it easy to open the hidden gates and allow everything to be exposed. His love makes it safe to begin to love yourself.

Sometimes I wonder what goes on in Peter's head that allows him to know what goes on in someone else's head!

I had just finished reading a beautiful book and was anxious for more. I thought that, perhaps, Peter might have something for me to read, so I decided that the next time I saw him I would ask. At that very moment I heard footsteps upstairs and down came Peter. He handed me a book and said, "Will this do?" He laughed, his eyes twinkling, and back upstairs he went.

Love knows all. And as often as I've wished I could do something about it, there isn't anything you *can* do about it except -- accept and love yourself.

Lightning

Some do not see you
My beautiful Lion of God.
Yet you dance right before them,
Shooting sparks of lightning
Into our eyes.

Are they blind or sleeping?
Suspecting every move,
Fearing every trick,
And weighing every statement
Against a leaden heart.

You laugh
And twist away
And then you're gone!
They grasp at
Empty air --

Poor blind ones.
It is not so hard
To love you
To belong to you
And follow in your Light.

It is not so hard
To let it all go

For the chance
Of a glance or a smile
From the fires of your heart.

What joy it is
To see you
To love you
To know you

Your eyes are
Shooting lightning
Into ours.

During one Sunday meditation, the wind was blowing fiercely: the trees were swaying, and the chimes were ringing wildly. Peter began to talk about peace and quiet. Suddenly there was complete silence; not a sound could be heard inside or out. The wind ceased, the trees stood still, and the chimes were quiet. It was as if the whole world had suddenly held its breath, and as if a saintly presence had entered the room.

Peter later described the heightened awareness that we all experienced as "a gift from the invisible world."

After meditation, we all sat round the great fireplace, mellow and relaxed. Ann brought us wine in delicate little glasses, and we savored each moment along with the wine. Moments like these are precious -- moments to listen, to watch, to be alert and awake.

Peter talked to us for a while on a number of different topics. At one point, when he spoke of "crumbling religions," a huge log fell out of the fireplace!

A little later he spoke of the idea of living on top of a mountain for several years with just his violin. Again, as soon as he spoke, the violin (which was laying on the piano bench) responded enthusiastically: one string singing out without being touched.

"Just a coincidence," a skeptic might say, but to be there, to feel the energy, and to see and hear these occurrences right on cue, is to know that this is no coincidence. Everything is *always* right on cue, and we sit in wonderment. It is a drama *extraordinaire,* where even inanimate objects play their part in the ongoing recital of Divine Force manifesting itself.

Peter helps me remember love. It is so familiar and yet so unlike anything I've ever felt in my life: a combination of all the good feelings I have ever experienced. All the happiness, all the hugs, all the sweet tears, all the warmth of a lifetime combined at once to make a flame of pure unconditional love. I didn't recognize it at first. I only know that being with Peter and learning from him makes me feel more whole and happier than I've ever experienced.

With the touch of love, all things are possible.

I recall so many times when Peter would transform and heal those suffering hurt and pain with just a touch of his hand and heart.

My brother Ned was visiting and we had gone on a very long hike in the mountains. Ned was limping toward the end because his knee had swollen and was causing him a lot of pain. Once back at Mystic Mountain, we went out back to enjoy the luxury of just sitting. Peter was asking questions about our journey and noticed Ned rubbing his knee. He asked what was wrong, and Ned told him his knee was sore. Peter went over and shook the knee in a friendly gesture, saying, "I don't think it will bother you anymore." And it didn't!

Peter did the same thing for a policeman friend of ours. We met him because of a sign we had put up advertising wood for sale. He came over to tell us that the sign did not comply with city codes, but that he wouldn't report it since it wasn't a hindrance to anyone. He lingered a moment, then said casually, "By the way, my shoulder has been awfully sore." He raised his arm and rubbed his shoulder joint as though to prove it was sore. Peter and I looked at each other and smiled. Obviously, the police officer had heard of him. Peter walked over to him and placed his hand on the shoulder, shook it in a friendly way and said, "I don't think it will bother you anymore." Years have gone by, and the officer says his shoulder hasn't been sore since.

Sometimes Peter's touch can be more dramatic. A young man came to the Mountain late one night. He was completely out of control. Totally hysterical. He desperately wanted to talk to Peter. I tried to get him to calm down and get some rest so he would be more sensible when he saw Peter. But he continued to cry and carry on, so I gave up and went to Peter to tell him the situation. Peter came into the room, walked over to the young man, and tapped him on the head. The young man went out cold. Peter smiled and said he'd see us in the morning. The young man awoke the next day and said that he hadn't felt as well for as long as he could remember. Oh, the touch of love!

Peter's touch works on plants as well. Our mimosa didn't open one day and was showing signs of dying. Peter went up to it and started talking to it. He whispered "sweet nothings," caressed its branches and within minutes the leaves were unfolding.

Oh, the touch of love! People, animals, plants -- we all respond to the touch of love. The healings are incredible; Peter's love is the miracle.

With the touch of a Master Gardener, all growth is accelerated.

One Sunday in February, we arrived for meditation to find a beautiful azalea next to Peter's chair. It was a mass of white buds. A few had already opened and others were opening in front of our very eyes. The week before, there hadn't been a single bud on the plant, yet seven days later it was reaching full bloom. As the meditation progressed, the blooms continued to open. At one point, Peter talked directly to the plant, and we gasped as one of the boughs jumped up dramatically!

The azalea bloomed magnificently for weeks after that. Everyone underestimated the number of blooms -- we kept track as they fell off and there were over 800!

Once in the spring, when we arrived for meditation, Peter showed us an acorn that he had picked up in the yard that morning. The acorn had started sprouting in just those few hours. He began the meditation by pointing out that we are all like acorns: we have as much potential to develop and transform as does the acorn to develop and become a mighty oak. About halfway into the meditation, Ann sighed with delight -- the acorn sprout had grown at least a half inch in that half hour!

This Master Gardener also attracts a garden of flowering people. He drops seeds within our hearts, waters them with his love, and shines on them with his light. Peter helps us to become strong, mature fruit-bearers who can weather adversity and flourish amongst weedy obstacles. Around Peter, the Master Gardener, no matter what the season, there is blooming and harvest (and his plants do pretty well, too!).

Just when I think I know Peter, and I think I know what to expect, I'm fooled again. To be around Peter is to learn how to open your heart and not hide your own beauty. Not only does the pain and hurt of the past begin to fall away, but the love and laughter of the inner child begin to blossom. Literally, one cannot hide from Peter, not even when dreaming.

Peter had lain down on the bed to rest. I heard him laughing as if someone were tickling him; then I saw a mouse jump out from under his beard! As it turned out, the mouse had been chased by the cat and had sought refuge in Peter's beard.

Oh, how many of us seek to be that close!

Peter has an uncanny way of making simple things profound and serious things light. He creates situations that force one to be introspective to achieve self-understanding. He is a tease and master of games. It's easy for *him* -- he knows what you're thinking! He knows what you're going to do next, so he can create fun (and sometimes not-so-fun) dramas.

One of the fun ones still amazes me because of how Peter obviously knew what my reaction was going to be, and because of the timing. I used to like to meditate by staring at a crystal hanging from a string. One evening when I stepped out of my room, Peter snuck in and doused my crystal with powder. Figuring Peter was the prankster, I just cleaned and polished the crystal. The moment I finished polishing it, it fell from its string. At the same time, I heard Peter roar with laughter in the other room. In a moment he was at my door, laughing. His eyes were all a-twinkle and on his face, a childlike grin. He said, "Jaya, when you clean and polish yourself, you will also fall off your string." More laughter. The setup was cute, but it brought about some deep thought.

Quite often people seek Peter out for advice and personal consultations. In most cases he prefers that the sessions not be recorded. But when a visitor insists, he has some unique methods of getting his way.

One woman who came for counseling showed up on time with her tape recorder in hand. Peter told her politely (obviously too politely) that he preferred not to tape the session. She informed him that she had bought the recorder just for this occasion and proceeded to set it up anyway.

Peter began to talk with the woman and she turned on her new recorder. It let out a deafening screech. She fumbled with it, turned it off, apologized, and tried it again. Same thing. She couldn't figure out what was wrong with it. She said it had worked perfectly in the car just before she came in. She wasn't able to record the session.

After she left, Peter said, with a mischievous smile, "I told her I didn't want it recorded."

Peter was giggling. Giggling in a silly way over some private joke. You know, the way children do when they find some little thing they think is screamingly funny. I watched him in amusement, then amazement as his giggles grew into fits of laughter. He was enjoying himself immensely, acting like a clown. I felt a twinge of disapproval. What had become of his composure, of his dignified demeanor? When they say mystics are fools, is this what they mean? The wild mirth continued as I grew impatient, thinking that the least he could do was share it with the rest of us. But by then he was uproariously out of control, holding his sides, slapping his knees. *Next he'll be rolling on the floor,* I thought, *and I'll bet he won't even tell us what's so funny.*

I ask you, how can you take a person like that seriously? Or yourself?

"Would you make it snow?" we asked one Sunday. "What kind of snow would you like?" replied Peter with a giggle signalling it was time for fun. "Do you want a white-out, a snow-stopper, or a snow that leaves by noon?" Our opinions varied and the working folks won with a vote for "snow on the ground but not on the roads."

I left that evening filled with laughter and love. I had no more thoughts of snow until I looked outside the next morning and saw snow piled on the ground, but none covering the road.

Peter can be an outrageous tease! It was the funniest scene, watching him huffing and puffing at those high, out-of-reach candles on the fireplace wall, and not being able to get them blown out. He caught us all on that one! After Peter's few "unsuccessful" attempts to blow out the candles, a group of about ten of us counted to three and blew. Even the ten of us couldn't blow them out.

As we all stood back, one of those *gaps* happened. One of those gaps in time where, if you blink, you miss. Those gaps are like doorways through which you can catch a momentary glimpse of the great cosmic "Ah-ha!"

Peter walked to the base of the fireplace and pretended to blow, but didn't . . . *gap* . . . the candles went out simultaneously, all six of them that were spread over an eight-foot distance!

Peter let out a roar of laughter. He had successfully caught our attention, then zapped us with his playful creativity.

Sometimes in one of those *gaps* with Peter, if you let your rational mind rush in, you can explain away what's taken place -- almost. But there will still be that undeniable feeling that something really weird just happened.

I was on the phone long-distance with Peter, discussing an intense telephone conversation I'd just had with a friend who had been quite negative and hostile. Peter said, "You know what I do in situations like that?" I said "What?" He said, "I say . . . *gap* . . . click." During that "gap" the power went out. My house became dark and quiet, *really* quiet, in stark contrast to the sunny day out the window. The power surged back on -- lights, refrigerator, clocks, etc. -- just as Peter said "click." I felt power surge through my entire body at that moment as well.

My rational mind tried -- unsuccessfully -- to dismiss it as coincidence. I knew for certain at that moment that Peter had deliberately added a little emphasis to make his point -- and to "empower" me in dealing with such situations!

We had a special "pizza party" at the Mountain to celebrate the anniversary of the Harmonic Convergence.

Everyone, including Peter, of course, was feeling very playful, and we suggested that he make a miracle happen -- like creating some wine. Amidst a lot of laughter, Peter got up and, with a flourish, poured wine out of his finger. It was a lighthearted game, but for those of us (myself included) who had not seen such a thing before, it was amazing!

When the wine finally was poured for everyone (from a bottle this time), an extra glass was placed at the end of the table where no one was sitting -- no one that we could see, that is. Slowly, through the evening, the wine disappeared from the glass. No one touched it, and it was in full sight of the entire group.

Peter also did a "napkin trick" for us. Somehow a torn piece exactly fit the corner of Ann's napkin.

Why does Peter do all these "tricks" for us? Though they are always playful, lighthearted and spontaneous, there are reasons. "Tricks" plunge us into questioning reality and allow us a glimpse into the vast freedom and mastery that Peter seems to have over everything. "I want you to be as free as I am," he says. My heart sings, knowing that there is so much more to life than the concrete reality we all know and -- hmmm -- love?

Peter's world is much more fun, and his dearest wish is for us to be a part of it.

Peter has great moves that are like "spiritual judo." When discussing a problem or concern, he is so loving and supportive. Then, when you least expect it, he'll turn around and kick you in the butt about the same issue. That is when my heart bursts with love for this man who loves us all so much. And I smile to myself and think, "Boy, that was beautifully done."

I had never had anyone "read" me before, but I had heard other folks talk about it. So one day I went to Peter for a reading. He read me all right . . . past, present, future and then some! He uncovered parts of my past even I had forgotten. Two weeks earlier I had given up eating meat after visiting a slaughterhouse. During my reading, Peter read the poem "Song of Peace" by George Bernard Shaw (a poem of tenderness toward animals). I was so deeply moved that tears of love and sadness poured from my eyes. To see the contradiction -- the lie I had been living and what I had been doing with my own body -- became clear for the first time in my life. Only with pure love could Peter have helped me to see myself.

Peter touched me in a very lighthearted -- and yet profound -- way, the weekend I was visiting the Mountain and wrestling privately with the idea of moving to Gatlinburg. I asked Peter about a particularly deep line on my palm -- he said it related to a traumatic family incident when I was in my late-teens/early-twenties. He said, "I could tell you more about it, but we don't need to get into that" or something like that.

I went into the kitchen and recalled the incident I knew he was referring to. He stuck his head in the window and said playfully, "July 27th, you were 19."

How exciting that he knew exactly when, and obviously what, had happened! Ann looked at me anxiously -- she said, "If that's not enough to send you into a healing crisis!"

About a month later I was living in Gatlinburg, to be closer to this amazing man who knew me better that I knew myself.

Peter was reading my palms. He asked me to open my hands and lay them palms up on the desk. He put his thumb in the center of my right palm and held it there several minutes. When he took his thumb away, a blister formed. After the blister healed, a red spot stayed on my palm for several days. I found out later that the blister had occurred on the line of fate. As the years pass, I see how my life course -- my fate -- was altered that day.

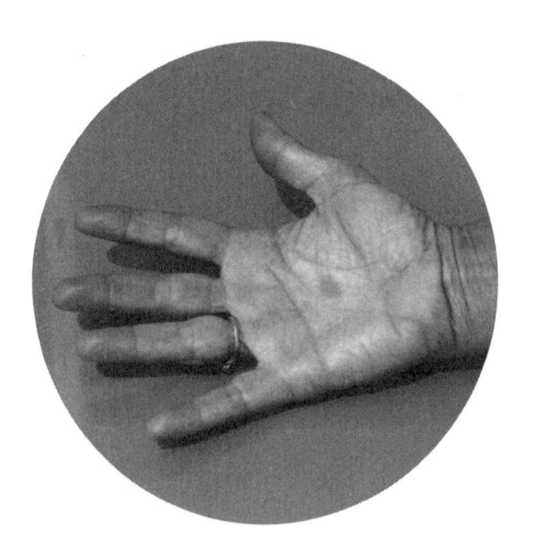

Peter "blew my mind" by reminding me of a drama that occurred while I was living in Colorado three years ago. He mentioned that it had happened by the stairs in the house I had been living in. "Ah, but there were no stairs in that house," I replied, as it was a ranch-style house. Then I remembered that there *were* two stairs in the middle of the living area . . . and then I had a vivid recollection of the incident to which he was referring. It had happened either before, or just after, meeting Peter for the first time.

Three years down the road and so much closer . . . and still sometimes I pretend he doesn't know everything about me! But, you know, it's wonderful. It is completely safe to be known.

I fell on some steps and badly hurt my tail bone. When I called the Mountain for some healing energies, the playful message came from Peter that he had "kicked me in the butt," but that, yes, he would send healing energies. The intense pain left almost immediately after receiving the message.

First the Zen stick, then the balm . . .

How do you tell a person who has been blind from birth what a beautiful, colorful sunset is like? It would be impossible to truly relate the color and splendor of a beautiful sunset to a blind person. Words can't describe it adequately. To know the sunset, one needs to see, feel, and experience it for oneself. I feel the same about Peter. My words are inadequate to describe the beauty, the splendor, the joyfulness and the unconditional love I have experienced from Peter. In this lifetime (more than 50 years), I have never encountered anyone with so much love to give. Peter is truly a magical, mystical, indescribable person.

The first time I met Peter was at a seminar at Mystic Mountain. Peter continually expressed so much joyous love! I could see it in his eyes; his whole body seemed to radiate love and light; I could even *feel* a presence of love and peace. How different Peter and Mystic Mountain were from anything that I had ever experienced! I am an engineer, trained in science, and entrenched in the computer world of logic and reason. There is no way to explain what I saw and felt, but I knew without a doubt that Peter was a special teacher for me.

I sometimes hear the words "guru" and "master" associated with Peter. I have only a hazy idea as to what those terms mean, and Peter is neither of those for me.

Who, then, is Peter? He is a sincere, ordinary human being who has deciphered the rules of life. He is like an elder brother who freely shares his time and love to remind us of who we really are. He is a beautiful sprite who sings joyously, dances spontaneously, laughs like a child, and looks at life with a mischievous eye. His talents are varied. He loves music and plays both the guitar and a violin which he made himself. He loves to talk on many different subjects, speaks several languages, and is a remarkable poet. He is a voracious reader and has an incredible memory. He is an enthusiastic athlete: lifting weights, riding a racing bike and running. He is a fine artist -- his paintings grace the walls of Mystic Mountain. He loves nature: the sun, the forest, the animals; he is a beekeeper, organic gardener and expert herbalist.

That is the "everyday" Peter, but there is also the Peter who shares Divine Wisdom with us, the one who shares as much of the truth as we are able to comprehend.

He is a totally honest human being and a wonderful role model. Physically, he is the healthiest person I have ever met; mentally he is the sharpest, emotionally the warmest. He loves to surround himself with simple beauty. Yes, spiritually he has reached peaks that we do not yet comprehend, but if anyone tries to make him "special" he will immediately correct them and say he is a "most ordinary" individual.

Having said all this, the bottom line, the most important thing of all, is that Peter is the most wonderful friend a person could ever hope to have.

Peter has a way of encouraging people to think for themselves and to value their own life experiences. He does everything he can to sidestep dependence on his words. Our friend Bill expressed the essence of Peter's "game" perfectly one day. We were standing in a group when Peter walked up. Someone posed a question to him, and he answered it totally opposite to the way he had earlier that day. Then he slipped away.

We all stood there looking at each other in bewilderment. Then we started to laugh. It was the glory of seeing one of Peter's games in action, and the security of knowing that learning with Peter is an independent process. Bill said, "He changes his mind and what he says so much, it makes you have to think for yourself!"

Peter creates a challenge that invites us to think independently. The independent thinker is the dissident, the rebel. The independent thinker has no concern for critics or opinions. The greatest challenge is that the independent thinker is the free man. And that is what Peter does -- he challenges us to be free.

The depth of my friend Peter is unfathomable. There have been times when we have locked eyes, and his ocean of love has poured into my small vessel until I thought it would burst at the seams. At the bursting point, however, I have always looked away . . . still afraid of sharing myself totally . . . still not knowing what lies beyond my limited self . . . still feeling the anxiety of going someplace I have never been. But still, my friend Peter continually pours out his ocean of love to me, each time stretching the limits of how much I am willing to receive and how much I am willing to give.

CONCLUSION

WITH PETER

CONCLUSION
WITH PETER

Have you always been the Magic Man -- have you always possessed these Divine gifts?

PETER: That's a tricky question. Please bear with me, words can not adequately convey truthful meaning. First, there is never a time when you do not have "Divine gifts," as you put it. What is a gift? Is it not something that you did not have or possess, and that now from an outside source you have received? A Divine gift is not an act of receiving, but an act of discovering. It is that you have allowed yourself permission to see what you have always possessed.

Once you unveil yourself of demand, that life should be this way or that way . . . once you unveil yourself of the conditioning effect of other people's opinions . . . once you experience the exhilarating feeling of being a lamp to your own roadway, of letting your own heartlight guide you . . . you leave the training wheels behind. Then experience of just *living* is seen as a Divine gift. Fully participating in life is magic!

Possession is an obsession with madness. When a person is obsessed with certain opinions, doctrines and teachings about life, they have cluttered over their bright light. It is now shaded with the thoughts of others.

Can you see how easy it would be to stumble, trip and fall through life? The magic is gone or -- more accurately -- it is just hidden from sight.

Have you ever noticed that a child can be laughing and joyful watching a leaf being blown across the ground, or playing with pebbles -- tossing them into the air or into a pond? That innocent, reflective quality of the child's unconditioned mind is like the Kingdom of Heaven.

Is that why Jesus said that one must be like a child to enter the Kingdom of Heaven?

PETER: YES! And, if you will, note that his many illustrations of the Kingdom contain the element of discovery. If the "Kingdom is within," as he said, it is so easy to see what he was really talking about in those many parables -- "The Kingdom of the Heavens is like a treasure hidden in a field" -- "The Kingdom of the Heavens is like a mustard seed . . ." -- "The Kingdom of the Heavens is like leaven hidden in three jars of flour . . .," or the parable of the pearl of high value.

What happens in all those metaphors? The treasure is found, the mustard seed grows to unimagined growth as a tree, the leaven expands and the pearl is discovered. Isn't that just like our consciousness? It has always been hidden right before us, then in a flash of insight we discover it; we take the covers off our light or *dis*-cover it. Simple, isn't it?

Then our consciousness is said to grow or expand, but it only appears to do so. It is the same as climbing to the top of a very high peak. Has the world expanded or has your vision? The pearl can be compared to your inner sight (though it is much more than that). First you discover you can see. You are no longer blind. Next you look around at the world and everything you focus on appears to expand. There is no expansion of consciousness. There is only consciousness and *un*-consciousness. There is blindness and seeing and sleeping and waking.

The "Divine gifts," the "magic," the "Kingdom of Heaven" are quite simply the dis-covery of yourself.

Peter, can you tell us -- What is the "self"?

PETER: Goodness, goodness! You'll just have to see that alone.

I can tell you that your name is Harry, Bob or Bill, Carol, Sue or Ellen, and if you have amnesia, you might believe me. But, when the amnesia breaks and is gone, it is not a matter of belief or teaching; you *just know* who you are.

At the most I might be able to trick you into remembering.

How do you do that? Will you trick me into remembering -- into my enlightenment?

PETER: O.K., the last part first. I will if you'll let me. Pulling Swiss watches out of the air and walking on water might get me a contract with Ringling Brothers and Barnum & Bailey Circus, but it has nothing to do with helping you discover who you are.

Hmmm . . . let's forget enlightenment, maybe we could become FAMOUS! I've got it . . . new names like -- "Maha Guru Houdiniji." I can see the billboards now, "Welcome to the world of watches and water." What a bargain -- a cheap wrist-watch, some holy water and amnesia just for coming to the show!

Peter, I asked if you would trick me into remembering, not into forgetting even more.

PETER: Oh my dear friend, isn't that what I was just doing? If I can point out all the ways not to go, all the ways of blind faith and all the confusing mazes -- the ego isle and the vanity vales, the psychic quicksand and guru gulch -- your leap into enlightenment becomes so simple, so natural, so intelligent.

Isn't it strange how quickly people get angry when you joke about *blind* faith? When people are so crippled that their salvation depends on an outside source -- wiggle their crutch a little and you will see all their anger surface. But, their anger is only an expression of doubt. A doubt that is so deeply hidden by the dark blanket of belief. One of my best tricks is to short-sheet you by challenging your beliefs. You try to go into a deeper sleep and you hear me laughing. Laughing even more loudly when you can't get the sheet over your head. Laughing again more loudly because you can't hide. Laughing even more with tears of love streaming down my cheeks seeing you've just jumped out of bed and are now wide awake. Yes, my dearest friend, we will laugh so hard the heavens will rock!

Doesn't faith have its place in helping us?

PETER: What kind of faith are you talking about? And what do you mean by "help"?

Well, I would say faith is a type of knowing that can help us become enlightened.

PETER: You are already enlightened. It is not a Christmas gift that Santa is bringing to you nor anyone else. You simply are not yet aware of your enlightenment. You cannot *become* enlightened.

Now this is dangerous talk because some ego maniac will hear this and proclaim himself a great master. This type of nut only has illusions of grandeur. They may *believe* or have *faith* in their being some chosen great leader, but if you dream you are awake how long do you suppose you will really sleep?

Faith can be a placebo or it can be based on facts. It is well-documented that a person can take a sugar pill and recover from their illness. That type of faith works very well for common miracles. In every area over which the mind can exercise control, faith and belief can make it happen.

There is a beautiful saying by Napoleon Hill of *Think and Grow Rich* fame. It is, "Whatever the mind of man can conceive and believe it can achieve." As far as the arena of thought is concerned, this is very true. I do not discount it in the least.

Now in the domain of consciousness, we enter the world of "no mind," as Zen masters call it. Faith and belief have never entered its gateway. Faith and belief can not even be servants in this kingdom. Faith is only needed by the unconscious.

Peter, are you enlightened?

PETER: I have been asked this question many times. Once I replied to a young man, "I have absolutely no idea what you are talking about. What do you mean by 'enlighten'? To me, that's just a vague word that people make a religion about. I've forgotten about that silliness years ago." The young man looked sad and disappointed. My heart ached for his confusion. So I said, "If you want the joy, the bliss, the freedom and the peace that I am . . ."

He left in search of great masters, hoping someday someone will give him the present with the big "E" in it and, of course, a bona-fide certificate proving his ENLIGHTENMENT. He never came back.

If the experience of enlightenment is as simple as you make it appear, why don't more people attain to it?

PETER: Because, the ego wants to make it difficult and hard so only the chosen ones, the faithful ones, can realize. This is absurd garbage! The sad, sick and pathological beg for trophies, awards and certificates. They need some jerk who doesn't have any idea of who they are themselves to approve them as teachers, masters, or avatars. This is a gross illness!

A beggar is always a beggar. It doesn't matter if you are begging for a dime or begging for somebody's approval -- it's still begging.

Why not be Lord of your world? Why not see yourself in your real glory, in dignity and self-esteem? Your natural self cannot be improved upon.

Is it then wrong to be a teacher and help others?

PETER: Help others! My God, these self-proclaimed "teachers" can't even help themselves. That's exactly the sickness I'm talking about. If you can convince enough other people to believe as you do, then you will have an excuse to believe yourself. This stupid worship of words can never lead you to the ultimate experience.

This type of teaching is only for gaining gold stars, a pat on the back and a "Now look at me. I'm worthwhile!"

Sorry folks, if you come here I will not lie to you. I will be so compassionate that I'll tell you the truth. You may not like it, and it may hurt, but it's the only thing I can do.

Because I love you to that degree, I promise I'll never allow you to make such a fool of yourself and reduce your dignity. Of course, you have total free will to avoid me forever.

Which has been the case with a few people. I loved them so much that I could not give my blessings to their delusions, to their lunacy. They feel very hurt when they realize that I have no diploma or trophy to give them. I have no bona-fide papers or certificates to give anyone. They feel very hurt that I am not the Messiah or the World Teacher or the Son of God come to Earth.

Why do they feel hurt?

PETER: Because, if I refuse to be special, a great Holy One, then they cannot brag or boast about their association with me. They cannot say, "My master is on the 33rd level of enlightenment" or "My master is the new World Teacher."

Do you think people will be impressed if you say, "Oh, Peter and I go hiking in the mountains together. He is my friend. He dresses in blue jeans or cut-off sweat pants and wears an old pair of running shoes."

No holy clothes. No special garb. And if you ask me my meditation it's probably lying in the sun getting a tan or lifting weights in my gym. No, I have not been sitting in samadhi for the last five years -- five seconds was enough. Why keep taking the medicine if you don't need it anymore? Oh, by the way, paralysis is not meditation.

Now people feel very hurt by all this. They want to feel as if they are so very special that the *Most Holy Reverend Maha Guru* has chosen them to sit with crowns on their heads at the right hand of God! What ego. What delusion! What nonsense! What a retardation.

The strangest thing of all is that people are very special, and also sometimes stupid, but that is perfect. I used to be more stupid than most. Do you make a beautiful flower more beautiful by decorating it with tinsel? It is perfect as it is and the more you do, the more you interfere, the less beautiful it becomes. It's like trying to grab a handful of water. The more you squeeze, the more it escapes your hold. Yet, the natural flow of water is so strong that in time it removes all obstacles in its way. When folks surrender to the current of the flow of life, life becomes an effortless joy. If you want to go to this shore or that shore, just a slight adjustment of your arm and leg positioning and you just glide right over. So easy, why make life such a chore, such a drudgery, such a battle? Just float with the energy and people will be saying, "Look at the magic, look at his miracles. He's special!" But, that is not the case. One simply becomes natural and perhaps, that's the specialness of it all.

The strange thing is that people continue to thrash about in the water -- they panic and drown. They become so obnoxious socially and domestically in trying to prove their worth. "I am the head of X.Y.Z. Company!" "I have a Ph.D." "I have 20 people working for me." "Look what I am doing to save the planet!" "I always put my family first." Oh, you poor self-sacrificing dear, look how righteous you are. Oh my, aren't you folks really important. Wow, we are impressed!

A rose does not make proclamations of its worth, nor does any tree, mountain or animal and yet, look at how we all are moved by their fragrance, beauty and majesty. Doesn't that tell us something?

Unnatural people always feel hurt and pain because they are always trying to prove themselves worthy by telling you how important they are.

When I say "be natural" I don't imply anything other than just being yourself.

Please do not behave in any conditioned manner. Do not be a robot. So many people teach that we are sinful, evil creatures, just like a bunch of rotten apples, bad to the core, and those people then expound on all the virtues we must develop to become pure. But, how can one build on rotten, sinful-material? Isn't that like the Proverb which speaks of building your house on a sand foundation? And if that is the case, why did God build with such material to start -- only to blame and condemn humankind as perpetually sinful?

Isn't it more sensible to see ourselves as already perfect from the source? If flowers, trees, birds and bees and all the animals on our glorious Earth cannot be improved upon, then humans also were not rotten apples from the start. Doesn't that make sense?

Then why the problem of sin and evil? Where did that come from? People do go to war and they do build bombs.

PETER: Yes, and that's the whole point. If we are already perfect when we behave according to our nature, then it is obvious folks are just behaving unnaturally. If they drop all unnatural behavior, there will be peace inside and outside.

What is unnatural behavior?

PETER: That's very simple -- it is any act done to comply with another's command that you dance to their music. It is in response to your fear of being disapproved, not liked or loved.

Unnatural behavior comes from feeling inadequate because someone has more knowledge, more money, more talent than you do. They may have a prettier wife or girlfriend, a nicer car, a larger house, and the list goes on and on.

The sickness is, "If I only had . . ." -- basically more approval. I say you are already approved; relax and you will find all your juices flowing -- all the love, peace, bliss and beauty. You will sing, dance and laugh out loud at your discovery.

It's ironic that we spend lifetimes groping about in the darkness looking for the light switch only to find it was never out of our hands. But, once found it is never lost again.

Peter, I understand what you just said about naturalness. There are many people who avoid unnatural additives in food, use no make-up and wear only natural fabrics. It also seems you enjoy natural clothing. Could you comment on this aspect of naturalness?

PETER: Some want to make a "religion" about what is natural or unnatural, and to those I say to go live naked with the monkeys of the jungle. I feel that's not the answer, but at least you wouldn't be a hypocrite to a religion of naturalness. Also, this is not to be confused with the natural state I refer to of just being yourself.

Don't we find pleasure in viewing a beautiful painting or other works of art? Cannot even the wearing of clothing become an art? Personally, I find that some women could present themselves more attractively by using a little make-up and perfume. Why look so sad and bland if it can be improved upon? I don't feel that's a sin.

This life is too good to miss. Celebrate this joyous opportunity of being in human form. Surround yourself with beauty, flowers, incense, song, dance, laughter and lots of warm, loving friends. This life's too good to miss! Please, there is no need to look like you are going to a funeral or just coming from one. Your joy can make this whole Earth a paradise just as your seriousness and sadness can make it a graveyard. The prophecy of the future is determined by how you live this very second.

You use a lot of satire in your speech. Why do you do that? I feel some people may miss the overpowering love we receive from you.

PETER: That's simple -- only intelligent people will understand what I am really saying. I do this all the time to qualify my audience. Stupid people are always the most easily offended. That shows they are still not ready for the spiritual adventure. With egos that large they couldn't get their heads through the door, so I quickly save them the trouble.

And why bother about me? I'm only for just a few people, a few friends. There are so many other places for folks to go. It's just amazing they even make a contact.

"Overpowering love" . . . Hmmm, that's only because you have come with an empty cup to an eternal spring. To you, the water is very sweet and healing and yet, oh how many cups there are that neither I nor those who come after me will ever fill. Do you think that you can do what a thousand messiahs have failed to do in the darkness of their tears? The ignorant one's cup is filled with empty dreams that leave no room for truth.

Peter, what is truth?

PETER: This very question was asked of Jesus by Pontius Pilate. Jesus remained silent, for he knew that the questioner must understand exactly what he is asking to truly understand the answer. "What is truth?" What is the question?

If what is asked is what is false or illusionary versus what is reality, then one is asking for an experience. The only response is silence, or as Lao Tzu, when forced to answer, replied, "The Tao that can be spoken is not the eternal Tao."

If a sleeping person asks in his dream "What is truth?" and an awake person hears, will he answer? Even if he says, "It is to be awake," does it have any value?

Now, if I slap you on the head with my bamboo stick and it wakes you up, you will reply "Ah this" and joyfully go on your way. Then the answer has been received.

Then can we assume that truth is enlightenment? And can this state ever be lost?

PETER: Beware that if you make any type of assumption you don't make an ass . . . of yourself. Ass is the first part of any assumption. Never assume anything. Just keep an open mind and you will know from your own personal experience the truth. You need no guide book nor even people like myself. The only help I can be is to confirm your direction of travel. There is, of course, no need to decorate the sign post. Sign posts are just sign posts. But, unless you have a very keen sense of direction, you may wander aimlessly for lifetimes. And yes, I can confirm your experience, but for what reason? This state of blissful being can never be lost. I've tested it many times over the years. I've tried in many ways and it just wouldn't go away. Oh well, what can I do? Hmmm . . . magic . . . it is just magic!

What is that, Peter?

PETER: LIFE! Life is magic. A phantom used to live in this house. That's before life entered the door and turned the lights on. Oh, my beloved friends, it will happen to you also. What can I say, there are only laughter and tears. Your worry of a thousand years will soon be gone.

If I can hold you close to my heart you will never hurt again.

Can I?

(Peter is now dancing and singing the *Magic Man* song)

Peter . . . ?

PETER: Yes?

What is that you are singing?

(still dancing and singing)

PETER: "Did you know there are people so alive,
when your heart feels them,
something bursts inside.
And suddenly you know
all you ever hoped for is true.
"When you're ready too,
it will happen to you,
more than just a few
will meet the Magic Man."

(silence)

This love in my heart is a fire . . . it will wipe every tear from your eyes. Never again will you shiver alone in the cold. The magic of this love, the magic of this moment, is simply a joy untold.

You are the magic. You are the gift. You are all there is and more. If you permit me to show you that, you will feel me as your very heartbeat.

What more can I say?

"I'm the Magic Man
doing all I can
to help the magic arrive.
"I'm the Magic Man
and I know I can
help your heart come alive."

THE BEGINNING . . .

SPECIAL EPILOGUE SECTION

Ten years have passed since the first of the enclosed adventures were experienced. In this new printing of THE MAGIC MAN, Peter has chosen to share with you a special message. We hope that you will find it "enlightening"!

EPILOGUE

FROM BEACH TO SHINING MOUNTAINS AND BEYOND

The sunny beaches of Fort Lauderdale are now shaded in a blur of time. It was the early nineteen eighties just a moment ago. Isn't it funny what happens in a blink of an eye? Excuse me while I check to see if I've tracked any sand on the carpet. Oh yes, I must not forget the aloe for my nose. So, you think I am kidding do you? And you've read the Magic Man and adventured with me a bit thru these pages? Hmmm...

Wasn't it yesterday we were walking down the beach together? Was it not then that I heard your heart utter the plea to be free? Wasn't it just yesterday, when you cried out in frustration and screamed in your mind that life wasn't fair? And when I laughed at you, you couldn't contain your emotions. And when I danced before you and shouted with joy that, "life is magic!", all you wanted to do was flee from me.

The past ten years are now condensed into paper and ink and squeezed between the covers of this beautiful book.

Ten years of sunrises and sunsets. Ten years of opportunities. From beach to shining mountains, thru a sea of ten thousand faces, are you still looking for the traces of your long forgotten home? What if I told you, you looked in all the wrong places?

If you don't know what you are looking for, I guarantee that your search will be endless. If you are a pandering servant seeking a master to serve, then I advise you to burn this book and move along. Ah ha! But, if you are that courageous fledgeling looking at blue sky, from your nest on high; I promise to push you hard, so you may fly alone. If you expect me to grow wings for you or forever feed you, I will call you fool.

If you expect to soar freely and effortlessly, I will applaud you. I will celebrate your wisdom. I will honor your display of courage. I will dance for your joy. And when you spread your eagle wings, glistening white in the light of the sun, soaring high above united as one with earth and sky, I shall point and say; see there flies the awakened one! I will call you god.

Oh, weary traveler, have you not yet tired of your endless search? If you have not found it yet...hmmm, could it be it doesn't exist, or could it be that you simply took the wrong path? Why do you continue to look on the outside for what you have misplaced on the inside? Are you retarded or just deceived?

How long do you suppose it will take the narcotic effect of your holy books, saints and devotions to wear off? How is it possible that the pleasures of unconsciousness can be that alluring? If a person fakes reality by living a fantasy, how many lifetimes will it take to awaken? My friends, don't hold your breath, there is no saint, holy book or devotion coming to the rescue. There is no one coming to do for you, what you must do for yourself.

Of course, there is no urgency to come to me as thousands have already done. I have no enlightenment to give you. The kingdom you seek is in your very own being. If you are foolish enough to ask someone to give you enlightenment, then remember, that what can be given can also be taken away. As a matter of fact, I am quite proud of undoing the "enlightenment" of many who come here.

May I tell you a story? I promise to make it up as we go along. There once was a man; a very dry, grouchy man. He was very serious and thus he never smiled [serious people rarely do]. He was abrasive and unpleasant and yet, he didn't mean to be. He had spent a lifetime in the pursuit of enlightenment, happiness and peace. Many of the grim faced spiritual teachers and their students that have come here out of curiosity, could have easily passed for this man's twin. I believe you also have had occasion to meet these people. Who of us has not seen the plastic smiles and caught the creepy smell of self-righteousness?

I have made this observation [now bear in mind that this is only a personal observation based on my own experience]; that long term meditators appear to display a certain bitterness toward life. Now, under no circumstances, give up meditation because of what I've just said. Allow me to make my point before you close the book. Hmmm, ...perhaps, I just made the point.

Have you heard about the man who was angry because he couldn't get the termites out of his house? Most long term meditators can't get the bugs out of their heads; thus the fires of anger flare at the slightest provocation. They sit, sit, sit and fail, fail, fail. Then they fake it. To live well in the eyes of others is more valuable to some of them, than truth. With many years of backlog reminders of failure, how could they adopt any other attitude? Obviously, they spent years using the wrong technique.

Now don't misunderstand, I'm not against waiting for a harvest. I don't believe one should dig up their seeds to see if they are growing. But, the question remains: how many springtimes are you going to let pass - when there is no evidence that anything is growing?

So, now we have this man with the foreign sounding name [which he gave to himself]. Of course, this name is not as exotic sounding as Peter, John, James or Mary. He is called, Mr. Namaste. His friends called him "Nasty" for short. Okay, if you like, I'll use his nickname. Nasty seemed to offend almost everyone he ever met. He always wanted to read your aura; tell you all the things that were wrong with you. Then he would explain how he could use his special powers to heal you. Of course we all knew not to ask him about his pasty complexion, his bloodshot eyes or the prodigious mound of flesh that he carried around his waist like a life preserver. He was always talking about things that no one could prove. Great masters appeared to him; 1,000 year old sages spoke thru him. He alone was picked to be a commander by General Chaos to head the flying saucer fleet [thanks Hal]. And, of course, his master was a 33rd degree on the level of enlightenment. Naturally, he was first in line to pay his $9.98, or was it $9,980.00? Oh well, I guess it doesn't matter. That was to pay for receiving the here-to-fore-hidden, sacred, secret mantra. Can you believe, with all these things going for him, that poor Nasty was still unhappy?

I really don't know what it was about old Nasty that I found so lovable; he was such an airhead and liar. A pathetic event takes place after so many years of seeking approval and repeating the unprovable as factual truth. It is, that when a lie is repeated often enough, with emotional fervor, it becomes a truth in your own mind. It is at that point that the capability to know truth is lost. It takes many years of intense intellectual honesty to develop the ability to think in a clear and rational manner. Honesty clears the clouds of confusion away so that "in-light-en-ment" may be discovered.

One day I said to Nasty: "why don't you just drop it?"

"Drop what?" he replied.

"All the things you have no proof for. Could it be that all your metaphysical questions are just an excuse for not being conscious? Could it be that your religious assumptions are drugs that prevent you from being honest, happy and awake?"

Well, judging from the look he just gave me, one would have thought I had just kicked the crutches out from beneath a cripple attempting to cross a busy street. Nasty forced a smile and huffed off mumbling something about demon possession and karma.

Many years have since passed. Then one day I received an unexpected phone call from Nasty. He explained that his entire life had undergone a powerful change. He even found a few honest and genuine friends and was happy for the first time in his life. I knew something was up since he didn't give me any - bless you brother; it's really up to connect with you on your astral power vortex. If you ever get balanced and clear enough to ascend to the violet mother-ship frequency, we'll network together. The "Counsel Of Nine" sends you blessings. Yo! I'm off to find my inner child's vision quest stuff. Astounded, I asked Nasty what happened to him. The smell of freshly baked bread is the same around the world; I could hardly believe it had happened to Nasty.

He answered in a gentle, reflective tone of voice. "Peter, about a month ago I celebrated my eighty third birthday. Everybody was enjoying the party but me. I went out on the back porch by myself and thought about the fact that I might not have many more birthdays to celebrate. I thought about the day many years ago when I burned with anger at your saying, 'why don't you just drop it? ...all the things that you have no proof for.' It was at this past birthday party, that I realized I have spent my entire life afraid of honestly admitting 'I didn't know'. I was living a pretend reality; the weight of that was simply too heavy to bear. I spent my life seeking saints, saviors and masters; in hope that they could give me a short cut to happiness. The burden of the fruitless chase was so oppressive at age eighty three, I chased my students away and gave it up that I might enjoy, at least, my few remaining years in what some might call 'selfish pleasures'.

"It was several weeks later, after digesting that I no longer needed to know about the afterlife, past lives, gods, angels and ancient civilizations [not that I wasn't curious] but, now I realized that those things would take care of themselves. I felt a great sense of relief and freeness inside. My questions were not answered, it was better than that - they dissolved. The grass is now so alive and much, much greener. The sky is so much brighter and bluer. I am so alive, so much at peace, so free, and oh, so happy! I am free to live in the moment, and that is where I found eternity." As he finished, he started laughing as he said: "we may never meet again or speak to each other, but, today I spoke to myself for the first time."

As I returned the receiver to it's place, the echo of an awakened man's laughter was still ringing in my ears. At that point, I smiled to myself and silently uttered in my heart: "life is magic and this moment, the key. Who will be next to awaken?"

I want to thank you for travelling with me from Fort Lauderdale to Mystic Mountain, from beach to shining mountains and hopefully beyond, thru the pages of this book. I hope I made you laugh [only the authentic can]. I hope your intelligence revealed to you how silly and absurd some ways of living can be. I hope you caught that sense of ridiculousness. I hope I made you cry, not tears of sadness, but, tears of joy from a sunburst of love from my heart to yours. I hope your wings are a little stronger now. But, above all things, I hope I made you fly...so my work may be done from beach to shining mountains and beyond.

LUMINOUS LIFE AND LOVE!

PETER